A Lifetime of Poetry

A Lifetime of Poetry

Lou S. Davidson

Copyright © 2009 by Lou S. Davidson.
Front cover art copyright © by Lou S. Davidson.

Library of Congress Control Number: 2008911453
ISBN: Hardcover   978-1-4363-9188-7
             Softcover   978-1-4363-9187-0

All rights reserved. No part of this book may be reproduced or transmitted in any form or by any means, electronic or mechanical, including photocopying, recording, or by any information storage and retrieval system, without permission in writing from the copyright owner.

This book was printed in the United States of America.

Front cover art is the author's original design entitled *Paul's Hibiscus*. Please see page for the poem this tropical flower inspired.

Back cover art is also the author's original design entitled *Splendor in the Morning*.

The other sketches scattered throughout the book are taken from the author's portfolio of line drawings collected during her forty-five-year career in china painting and watercolor artistry.

All scripture passages are taken from the King James Version of the Bible.

To order additional copies of this book, contact:
Xlibris Corporation
1-888-795-4274
www.Xlibris.com
Orders@Xlibris.com

Dedication

To my precious family,
my sixth grade teacher who
taught me *how* to write poetry,
and to Jesus Christ,
my Savior and Lord.

AUTHOR'S BIOGRAPHY

I was born on October 31, 1920 on a farm outside of Trenton, New Jersey. I had an older brother and sister, Willa and Delmar, Jr. then, after eight years, we had Le Roy, Vera, Leslie, and Irene Shirley. We all married and had our own families except Irene, who went to be with the Lord as a baby. (See "THE LOST POEM").

At 18, I graduated from High School, the first in the family to do so, and married Earl L. Smythe in 1938. We lived in Lambertville, N. J. and he worked in a hosiery mill. Then the mill moved south and we moved to Harrisburg, PA. I found work in the BELL and he went to work at an Air Base in Middletown. He wanted to enlist in the NAVY, but worked in and "Essential" Industry where they serviced the planes after 50 Missions over Germany.

One day he came home and held me in his arms and said: "I want you to give your two-weeks notice and quit your job. The war is going to be over, and we can buy our own home and start raising our family."

I worked at the Bell and I had written a 4-line poem about each of the "Pioneers" which would be read as they showed the baby picture of that man. They were so pleased as they tried it beforehand, and they invited Earl and me to be their guests at the ball. Of course, I had to have a gown, so I bought some white moire' taffeta and cut and sewed until I stood in front of the mirror, thinking "tonight's the night'! I'll give it one more pressing and Earl should be here any moment."

As I heard the door bell ring, I set down the iron, and went to the door. "Come in", I said then showed them to a seat saying, "Earl will home any moment now," and I went back to the ironing board. One man got up and came to me, took the iron out of my hand, and set it down, then "led" me to a chair and set me down.

He said: "There was a plane crash this morning," I blurted out: "OH—I heard that sputter and then it was gone." Then he said: "Earl was in that plane." He gave me time to comprehend it then he said: It was just a routine test flight, but there was one fellow who parachuted to safety. When we picked him up, he said: "I was the only one with children, and Earl was the only one who took a parachute, so when we knew we were in trouble, he took off his 'chute, put it on me, saying: "You have to raise those kids" and kicked me out of the plane."

After that, I joined the WAVES. I had a good job in the Statistics Dept. in Washington D. C.

When the war was over, I went to Miami, FL. and found the Lord as my Saviour, I asked Jesus to come into my heart, as Earl had tried to get me to do saying, "Lou, you have religion in your head, but you need Christ in your heart." I knew then that he was in heaven and that someday I would be there too. There, I met and married Ken Davidson, a returned Marine, with three more years of college, but we made it!

He was an Elder in the Church, and sang; I taught Child Evangelism Classes and was the Director of the North Miami Christian School until Dr. Kennedy started his School in the N. W. We gave him, our students, books, desks, etc., and I started to paint. I had classes in our home and became a member of the International Porcelain Art Teachers, Inc.

The Lord blessed us with three loving daughters, three sons-in-law, and grand children. We retired early, renting our store building for more that we were both earning, so we went and served as Volunteers at Wycliffe Bible Translators Home base in N. C.

We enjoyed our Grandchildren, and now, Kenny's with the Lord, but I'm enjoying the loving care of our Daughter Ginni, and Joe and my GRAND CHILDREN and GREAT GRAND CHILDREN.

I'll be forever grateful to the teacher who taught us to write poetry, I think it was in 6th grade, but now at 87 years of age, "still typing" but I can't think of her name.

ENJOY THE POEMS AND THE WRITINGS.

Contents

Love of God

Poems of Faith and Salvation

A Child's Choice 17
Believe! 18
The Guest Book 19
The Guest Book 20
Home in Heaven 21
Jesus Died for Me 22
Jesus's Love 23
Just Two Words 24
Lest There Should Be No Tomorrow 25
My Salvation 26
My Search for Salvation 27
Only You, Lord 29
Peace of Mind 30
Repentant Sinner's Prayer 31
Salvation, the Greatest Gift 32
The Invitation 33
The Creator's Love 35
Tickets To Eternity 36
Your Heart Will Live Forever 37

Poems of Praise and Prayer

A Firm Foundation 41
Before My Prayer Time 42
Choral Introit/Recessional 43
Count Your Blessings 44
Draw Me Nearer 45
Faith 46
God's Power and Love 47
Hallelujah! 48
He Holds My Hand 49
How I Love The Name of Jesus 50
I Praise Thee, Lord 51

My Prayer For Today 52
My Psalm 53
My Service 54
New Verse for a Child's Prayer..55
Of Smiles and Tears 56
Oh, Lord, Use Even Me 57
One Wish...58
Peace at Last 59
Start a New Day..60
The Banker 61
The World Gets in My Way 62
To Know Thy Will..63
To My Missionaries..64
Wait and Pray...65
Welcome to God's House 66

Poems of Testimony and Service

A New Road 69
God's Challenge...70
Finish the Job 72
His Servants...73
Just Imagine 74
Lord, Lead Me Today..75
On Giving..76
On Witnessing..77
Our Mighty God...78
Sow to Reap 79
The Death of His Saints 80
To Do or Not To Do 81
Use Me, Lord 82
What Would You Have Me to Do, Lord? 83

Poems of Hope and Encouragement

A Foolish Choice..87
Daydreams 88
Friday Morning 89
God Knows...90

I Have Seen the Christ	92
I Need another Miracle	93
Jesus Can	94
Jesus Said It	95
Not Go to Church?	96
On Fasting	97
On Smoking	98
Payday	99
Reclaiming Your Power	100
Rise to Glory	101
Telling the Way	102
Ten Minutes	103
The Ideal Christian	104
The Old Letter	106
The Picture	107
There Must Be More to Life	108
Today!	109
Walk by Faith	110
What God Can Do	111
You Didn't Ask	112

Love and Loneliness

Poems of Earl

The White Gown	117
I Think Of You	118
Our Monthiversary	120
My Little Engagement Bunny	122
Would You?	123
A Prayer	124
Our Fifth Anniversary	125
About Earl	127
No True Love Songs	128
Still Searching	129
To Earl in Heaven	130
I Found Peace At Last	131
Earl's Songs To Me	133

Being a Widow

I Miss the Missus	137
It's Spring Again	139
If God Had Given Me a Choice	141
June the Seventh	142
Diamonds and Opals	143
Evening	144
A Widow's Changed Life	146
Reading Psalm 61	147
My Guest	148

Poems of Ken

Someone New	153
My Angel	154
Ken's Valentine	156
Happy Birthday, Ken	157
Iron A Shirt	158
Homemade Valentine	159
It Just Takes Time	160
My Husband's Valentine	161
Looking Back	162
To Ken	164
Ode to My Hubby's Picture	165
Ode to My hubby, Ken	167
A New Beginning	168
The Tree Outside My Window	169
To Ken in Heaven	170
The Other Hand	171
Just One More Kiss	172
A Note to Ken	173
Kenny's Blessing	174
In Church	175

Love of Family

Our Three Girls and Grandchildren

Adopted Love	179

A Mother's Love 180
Joy's Sunday School Shoes 181
Donadeane's Healing 182
'Neath the Shadow of the Cross 184
Continue in My Word 185
For Ginni 187
The Story of Paul's Hibiscus 188
New Verse to an Old Hymn 189
Dearest Ginni 190
Reunion at the Horizon 191
Happy Birthday, Daughter 192
The Marriage Braid 193
Tiffany's Card 194
Happy February 14 to My Family 195
Sometimes Daddy Must Say No 196

Family and Friends

Dear Mother 202
Happy Birthday, Mother 203
Mother 204
Little White Church 205
Oh, Death, Where Is Thy Sting? 206
Loving Thoughts on Mothers' Day 207
To Mother Merritt in the Hospital 208
The Anniversary Plaque 209
The Lost Poem 210
Reminisce 211
A Heaven Without Children 212
A Friend Is Someone You Can Ask 213
The Surprise Gift 214

Love of Laughter

Fun and Fanciful

A B C Poem 217
And God Said 220
Bus Ride Through the Alps 222
Cherry Blossoms in DC 223
Green Apples 225

Shadows..226
The Budding Artist..227
The Maple Tree...228
The Solution..229
You're Just A Bird 230
Unlimited Potential 232
Little Rhymes..233

Love of Celebration

Poems of Christmas and Easter

Christmas at Our House......................................237
Christmas Celebration...238
Christmas Peace to You.......................................239
Jesus's Birthday..240
Merry Christmas NOT Merry "Xmas" 242
Our Christmas Message 244
The First Christmas Gift......................................245
The Gift of Christmas..246
The Good News 247
The Reason We Celebrate....................................248
The Story of Christmas 249
What Christmas Means to Me.............................250
After He Rose 251
Let's Celebrate 252
The Easter Story 253

Love of God

Poems of Faith and Salvation

A Child's Choice

Lou S. Davidson   © 2004

Children know of the crucifixion
That Jesus arose from the dead.
They have heard the many promises
And all the verses they have said.

They can write the verses on the board
Correctly spelling every word.
They know all about His promises
But the best have never heard.

They could ask Jesus into their heart
The Holy Spirit would come in
And bring peace and joy abundantly
Cleansing their souls from every sin.

The lingering fear and torment
Satan uses to make them fret
To keep them from accepting Christ
By saying, "They're not ready yet!"

Believe!

Lou S. Davidson   © 1949

So long I had been dead inside, my soul refused to sing.
My heart was deaf to Jesus's call but heard each *wordly* thing.
My friends were also of the world, temptation held full sway
And I was like so many folks who pass along life's way:

I had heard of my Redeemer, and His love so great for me,
And knew it was for my sins He hung on Calvary's tree.
I knew the Christmas story well; That He is the Son of God
I knew each parable He taught while on the earth He trod;

I knew that He arose from death and lives with God above;
That He calls the sinners to Him and offers them His Love;
I knew He is the Way between me and the Throne of Grace;
Through Him *alone* I can see my Father's holy face;

I knew I was a sinner and that I would be forgiven;
Each night, I said my prayers knowing God was in His heaven;
But now there is a difference that can hardly be conceived:
Before I only *knew* these things, but I never had *believed*.

The Guest Book

Lou S. Davidson   © 1993

"Welcome to my home," she said
      "I'm so very glad you came;
Will you take this little guest book
      And in it sign your name?"

I took the book and held it
      As I read the other names
But I thought, *I just won't bother*
      Let's start the fun and games!

"Thank you for coming" she said,
      My lonely hours to fill,
I have no other kin you know
      I'll name you in my will."

Death followed soon. Her bequest
      For her large estate to share
Was, "Go to my little guest book
      You'll find the names in there."

Jesus died for all the world
      Their sins to be forgiven
But only those in the Book of Life
      Will share His home in heaven.

Only you can make the choice
      But you can't afford to wait
For who can know tomorrow
      That may be just too late!

Just say, "Thank you, dear Jesus
    You died for all my sin;
I open my heart in prayer today
    And ask Thee to come in."

When you do, your name will be
    In God's own secret way,
Inscribed in the Lamb's Book of Life
    For that great Judgment Day.

The Guest Book

    I found the need when speaking to people about the Lord for something to leave with them, which they could read that would have the invitation for them to accept Christ as their Savior.

    The first part of the poem is make-believe, but the other part is the invitation. I have one in my purse at all times. For example, as I look on the racks for a new blouse or as I try on shoes, I hand one to the lady to read while she's waiting for my decision. After someone has read the poem and says they are ready to have their name in God's Book of Life, I just have them read the last two verses again. It really works. Praise the Lord!

Home in Heaven

By Lou S. Davidson   ©

Jesus died for all the world,
His heavenly home to share!

But only those in the Book of Life
Will find their home up there!

Jesus Died for Me

Lou S. Davidson

Barabbas was a wicked man
A murderer was he—
Condemned to die for wrong he'd done
But then he was set free!

For in his place went Jesus,
The Son of God Who came
The one who brought sight to the blind
And devils fled His Name.

So willingly He gave Himself
To take the sinner's place
That those who stood nearby His cross
Saw only love there on His face.

I too was such a wicked one
No good thing could I do.
Until one day, I heard Him say
That He took my place too!

For in my place went Jesus
To die that I might live
In peace and joy and happiness
And the Good News to others give.

Jesus's Love

Revelation 3:20
Lou S. Davidson   © 2005

"I love you," Jesus says,
"I died for all your sin.
Please open now the door
And bid me to come in."

O yes, Lord, please come in.
Holy Spirit, fill me,
Lead me, guide me, love me,
Help me live for Thee.

Revelation 3:20 says, "Behold, I stand at the door, and knock: if any man hear my voice, and open the door, I will come in to him, and will sup with him, and he with Me."

Just Two Words

Lou S. Davidson   © 2001

Two words can change your entire life!
Just say, "I do" and she's your wife!

Two words can free you from your sin
Jesus is knocking. Just say, "Come in!"

Two words enable you to receive
A place in heaven when you say, "I believe!"

Don't let the devil seal your fate
By making you wait 'til you hear "Too late!"

Lest There Should Be No Tomorrow

Lou S. Davidson   © 1995

Take that step into the future
If it's what God wants you to do.
Put out of your mind
the things behind
That drain all your strength from you.

Labor today for things that count
Bring joy to those who sorrow.
Trust in Christ today
for your destiny
Lest there should be no tomorrow.

My Salvation

By Lou S. Davidson   © 2001

It was one of those big-band dance nights,
He said, "May I have this dance?"
I realized on our wedding day,
That I wasn't there by chance.

Then as those happy years came and went
Our love grew right from the start
He said, "You have knowledge in your head,
Lou, but you need Christ in your heart."

Those happy years turned into seven
A flaming bomber took his life
I wondered, "Did he go to heaven?"
The thought that brought me inner strife!

Then one day in a little white church
I asked Jesus into my heart
Which Earl had tried to get me to do
Right from the very start!

Then I knew that he was in heaven
And some day I would be there too.
With that peace, came another husband
And my joy was renewed anew!

The next forty-three wonderful years
Our children and grandchildren too,
Have all asked Jesus into their hearts
And do what the Lord says to do.

    Amen!

My Search for Salvation

Lou S. Davidson   © 1992

"My husband is dead, blown up in a plane!
How can I know if I'll see him again?
Where is he now—in heaven or hell?
God speaks of both—Oh! how can I tell?"

    One said, "You truly are left in the lurch,
    Perhaps you will find the truth in the church."
    "But that cannot be," I said through my tears
    For I've been in church most all of my years."

    "Then talk to your folks for the wisdom you seek."
    "But Sunday to them is the same as the week!
    They say, 'Just be good'—and good we have been
    But God's holy Word talks all about sin"

"Then try somewhere else, or even try two."
I did, and my hopes were primed anew.
He told of heaven, its glory so fair
I thought, "Now he'll tell me how to get there."

    He spoke of pride and original sin
    And all that would keep one from entering in.
    My soul was so much under conviction
    Then he said, "Bow for the Benediction."

    Well, I won't give up—I'll try just once more
    But that day proved only worse than before.
    They all agree there's a heaven and hell
    But where is my Love—Oh how can I tell?

I'm so all alone—alone in my grief
What good is my life? Death could bring relief!
But then God had another plan for me
And rescued me from the dark, lonesome sea.

I went once again, the answer to find
A little white church—the people were kind.
The pastor said, "To get rid of your sin—
Just open your heart, let *Jesus come in.*"

  Then I prayed the prayer he helped all to pray
  And Jesus *came into my heart* that day.
  I remembered the time my husband had said,
 "You need Christ in your heart, not words in your head!"

Then I knew for sure that someday I'd be
 In heaven with him for eternity
  But my heart is burdened and always will be,
   For all those who knew—and wouldn't tell me!

Only You, Lord

Lou S. Davidson   © 1994

Dear Lord:

    Only you can make the sunshine
        And bring the gentle rain;
    Only you can make the wind blow
        And turn it off again!

    Only you can make the sea roar
        Yet keep it in its bound
    Only you can make the seeds grow
        For flowers all around!

    Only you could send your Son
        To die on Calvary
    Then raise Him up to life again
        To set the sinner free!

    Now He stands and is gently knocking
        Each heart He seeks to win
    But only *we* can be the one
        To ask the Savior in!

    Yes, only we can say, "I've sinned
        Come into my heart, I pray;
    Those nail-pierced hands are all I need
        To wash my sins away!"

Peace of Mind

Lou S. Davidson © 1950

The world in turmoil shakes its head;
Wars are raging, sons are dead!
Broken homes and crimes increase.
Where, oh, where can one find peace?

Books were written telling how
Was it gained? Where is it now?
Some sought power for joy within
Or planned on wealth, their peace to win.

Like others, I tried all of these.
Then in despair, fell on my knees,
Confessed my sins to God in prayer,
Accepted Christ and found peace there!

This poem was written when our country was involved during the Korean Conflict.

Having endured the Second World War before I was saved, I could relate to the turmoil and fear of the people during this time of war. I personally knew that God is the only one to give inner peace no matter what state the world is in!

Ken was a marine, and I served in the WAVES in World War II. We knew the price that was paid by those in military service, as well as their families. We prayed for those who had gone overseas to fight and for their families who waited for their safe return. We prayed too for the end of the war.

Repentant Sinner's Prayer

Lou S. Davidson © 11/30/86

Oh, God, my heavenly Father,
I come to thee in prayer.
I know that I'm a sinner
And saddened with despair.

But now I know you love me
Because of Calvary.
When Jesus bled and died there
I know it was for me.

Now I believe in Jesus,
Who paid for all my sin.
I open wide my heart's door
And ask Him to come in.

And as your Holy Spirit
Now fills my heart with peace,
I know I'm now your child
My life will never cease.[*]

So thank you, heavenly Father,
For saving me, and I pray
By thy Holy Spirit
I'll live for thee each day.

      In Jesus's name, amen.

---

[*] John 3:16: "For God so loved the world that He gave His only begotten Son, that whosoever believeth in Him should not perish but have everlasting life."

Salvation, the Greatest Gift

Lou S. Davidson

There is nothing I can be
There is nothing I can give
There's no work I can do
  For my salvation!

But God said I must believe
And His Son I must receive
For Jesus paid the price
  For my salvation!

Now everything I do
Now everything I say
Now everything I give
  Since my salvation

Is to show my love to Him
And seek other souls to win
That they might also share
  This great salvation!

The Invitation

By Lou S. Davidson   © 1978

I wandered into church one day
My soul to satisfy.
Not one said aught a word to me
As I passed on by.

The pastor spoke so glowingly
Of heaven and those who go,
But how to become one of them
I longed so much to know.

Then as my soul grew quiet
My fighting ceased to be
I longed to cross the border
And be saved eternally.

Those moments I remember now
Completely without friction
I was so close, but then he said,
"Receive the Benediction."

Then many years went crawling by
My anguished soul condemned
Each step going downward
I yearned for life to end.

So once again I sought a church
And the friendly folk that day
Awoke my yearning for the good,
And I heard the pastor say,

"If you would like to know the Lord
And of His heaven have a part
Then pray this prayer with me and ask
He'll come into your heart."

The very words he gave to me
My anguished troubled soul
Repeated them, and Jesus Christ
Came in and made me whole.

Now many years I've lived for Him
Joy has replaced the tears,
But I wonder who's responsible
For those horrid, wasted years.

The Creator's Love

Lou S. Davidson   © 1979

The earth is My footstool
And heaven is My throne.
Creation is allMine
And for My joy alone.
I've anchored every star
According to My plan
I control the universe
What need have I for man?
What need have I for man?

Yet He poured out His life
Unto death, for Your sin.
Will you open your heart
And let Him come in?
Just claim Him as Savior
He'll give you light and peace,
His love and His presence,
And a joy that will not cease;
And a joy that will not cease!

Tickets To Eternity

Lou S. Davidson © 1994

I've got two tickets to eternity
To that dreamed-of land above
Where tears and sorrows will be no more
And all is peace and joy and love!

I've got two tickets to eternity
They were freely given to me.
Would you like to have this extra one?
I'll gladly give it to you free*!*

I'm not sure when I'll be goin' there
But my place is reserved, I know,
For I know the one who paid my fare
And I'm trusting in Him 'til I go!

I would like to take you along with me
There's no other place the same,
Just put your trust in Jesus, my Lord,
And get a ticket in your own name.

Your Heart Will Live Forever

Lou S. Davidson @ 2006

God is searching every heart
He sees our every sin,
He's willing to forgive us
If we will ask Him in.

God is waiting every day
In our sinfulness, He sees us,
All we have to do is say,
"Come into my heart, Lord Jesus."

Love of God

Poems of Praise and Prayer

A Firm Foundation

Lou S. Davidson   © 1988

I am sealed with the Spirit
    I am safe and secure
It's a finished transaction
    All time will endure!

Now I know He is with me
    Freedom I've found!
With my sins all forgiven
    I'm no longer bound.

I know Christ as my Savior
    A gift of God's grace
To the praise of His glory
    Till I see His face;
To the praise of His glory
    Till I see His face.

When I Wrote "A FIRM FOUNDATION"
Lou S. Davidson

    As we get older and more and more of our friends go to be with the Lord, it makes one think how fragile our own life is. To know the Lord personally, praying every day and seeing the answers makes me know that He is with me and that someday I will be with him. Thus, I look at death as a blessing, not something horrible, and focus on what He would have me to do before I go.

Before My Prayer Time

Lou S. Davidson © 2004

Dear God:

These are not just names, they are people
I ask Thee for your blessing.
Some need many material things,
But all need your caressing!
That feeling of being close to thee
To protect them from all sin,
Others need your tender healing touch
And care for their loving kin.
Some need wisdom to perform your work
That the job might be well done!
Some may need a break—a special time
Just to have a little fun!
You know each one, you know every need,
You know their love for you.
And when I've finished and said "Amen,"
Dear Lord, please bless me too!

Choral Introit

By Lou S. Davidson

Come ~ bring your burdens
Though heavy they be
Come ~ bring your cares
And cast them on me.

Come ~ raise your voices
In anthems of praise
Come ~ I will bless you
And brighten your days.

Choral Recessional

Go in the comfort
Of strength and peace
Go in the knowledge
Of love ne'er to cease.

For lo ~ I am with thee
Thus saith the Lord.

Count Your Blessings

Lou S. Davidson   ©1993

The list of *my greatest blessings*
>Was marvelous to behold

And though the list grew very long
>Not one could be bought with GOLD!

So make a list of *your blessings*
>Things that fill your heart with mirth

And you'll see that God has made you
>The richest person on earth!

Then after you list your blessings
>If you want to have real fun

Take the time to pray to God
>And thank Him for *each one*.

One morning while having my morning devotions, I thought of the problems facing me that day: the main one—how to get a mortgage for a house I wanted to buy before I had a sale on the apartment I had. Money, money, money—it seems that everything is based on *money*!

Then my spiritual mind took over, and I realized that God had always worked out my problems, and He still would, so I started thinking of the things that really mattered.

I decided to make a list of my greatest blessings, thinking that my jewelry, apartment, money, etc., would begin the list. However, to my surprise, I found that by the time I had used up the piece of paper, I still had not listed any of them.

So I picked up a scrap of notepad and penned the poem. Later I found it was just the thing to use for a card that I was making for a couple's fiftieth anniversary.

Draw Me Nearer

Lou S. Davidson   © 1963

"Draw me nearer, precious Lord,"
I sang with all the rest.
I did not know He heard my prayer
Nor could I know the test.

I did not know He'd take away
All the things I held dear,
Yet these were things, which hindered
His gentle drawing near.

"I will serve thee, Lord," I said.
"What will you have me do?"
I prayed till tears ran down my cheeks
Before the task was through.

There followed pain and heartaches sore
Yet grace and joy are mine!
Till nearer, still, I long to be
I pray these words divine:

Draw me nearer . . .
        nearer . . .
                nearer . . .
                        Precious Lord.

Faith

Lou S. Davidson © 1994

The sun was well below the treetops
    But I knew 'twould soon be day
When one dark cloud just burst with light
    And the darkness rolled away!

Once again, God made the sun to rise,
    To set when the day is done
A daily proof of His *faithfulness*
    To those who will serve His SON.

I think back on the things of the past,
    How He answered every prayer.
By each daily sunrise and sunset
    He reminds me of His care.

    Rising before dawn, I opened the blinds and went out to open the east windows on the porch. The darkness seemed to ask me why I get up so early—one reason is that I love to see the sunrise! I can depend on it! It reminds me of the great and mighty power of God and His faithfulness. I also like to see the black trees of the silhouette change to green as they soak up the first rays of the sunlight. It reminds me that on the first day in Genesis, God said, "Let there be light" and there was light! Then I remember His mighty power and his faithfulness, and I'm ready to serve Him another day.

God's Power and Love

Lou S. Davidson   © 1996

For thou art mighty in power,
    But so tender in love!
You can cause a mighty earthquake,
    Or send rain from above;

Your knowledge encompasses all,
    You bind the mighty seas,
You set all the laws of nature,
    Yet break them when you please.

You hold the keys to heaven's gate
    And who shall enter in.
Yes, Lord, but there is one thing:
    You cannot look on sin!

By thy great love you made a way
    For all who would, to know
You gave your own begotten Son,
    Because you loved us so.

And as your mighty power we see,
    While we're still here below,
May we be used to tell of thee
    To others as we go.

Hallelujah!

By Lou S. Davidson   © 1973

I'm gonna talk with the Lord, hallelujah!
I'm gonna talk with the Lord today.
Since I've opened my heart
And let Jesus come in
He washed all my sins away.

I'm gonna walk with the Lord, hallelujah!
I'm gonna walk with Him all the way.
Though I still fail Him
He is faithful and just
To forgive me when I pray.

I'm gonna talk with the Lord, hallelujah!
I'm gonna tell Him all my cares
He tells me in His Word
He knows my every need
And I know He hears my prayers!
Hallelujah!

He Holds My Hand

Lou S. Davidson   © 1957

He holds my hand
When I'm happy and gay.
He holds my hand
When the day has turned gray.

He walks with me
Tho' the pathway be steep.
He keeps me near
When awake or asleep.

Surely he knows
And must understand
How much I need Him
To hold my hand!

One day on the way home from church, I thought

How I Love The Name of Jesus
Lou S. Davidson   © 1979

I love the name of Jesus
Oh, how I love to hear
A little child whisper it
When he bows his head in prayer.

I love the name of Jesus
I think it's just so great
When the choir's voices raise it
Till the rafters all vibrate.

I love the name of Jesus
But lo, it brings me pain
When I hear those reckless people
Take that holy name in vain.

I love the name of Jesus
When oh! So silently
I breathe it in my deepest need
And He gives sweet peace to me.

I *Praise Thee, Lord*

By Lou S. Davidson © 2001

There's food in the fridge
And clothes on my back.
For good things to do
There's never a lack.

My bills are all paid
And cash in the bank,
Car's running OK and
There's gas in the tank.

A church where I go
To worship my Lord
Friends to stand by me
In one sweet accord.

A family who loves me
And bring me such joys
We're three generations
With three great-grandboys!

People are praying,
God's in command.
He has us all in
The palm of His hand.

With plenty to do
And strength for each task
I just praise the Lord!
What more can I ask?

My *Prayer For Today*

Lou S. Davidson © 1952

Oh, God, our heavenly Father
I humbly seek thy face
In the name of our dear Savior
Who took this sinner's place,
Who washed away my guilt and shame
And keeps me in Thy care
With thanks for my salvation
And this privilege of prayer.

I thank thee that my Savior lives
That thou almighty art
Thy precious Word, my lamp, my guide,
For the peace within my heart;
For the loved ones thou hast given me
And a joy that never ends
For our home, our food, our freedom,
Fellowship with Christian friends.

I pray for thy disciples, who
Have gone from shore to shore
To spread the Gospel tidings;
And for those engaged in war.
Oh, may I lead some sinking soul
To trust in Christ today,
And give me strength for every task
In Jesus's name, I pray.
Amen.

My Psalm

By Lou S. Davidson © 1989

*The Lord is my shepherd,
Then why should I fret?*

*The Lord is my shepherd,
How could I forget?*

*He leads me and guides me
Each step of my way*

*And soothes me with peace
Whenever I pray.*

*The loved ones I cherish
Each need he has met.*

*The Lord is my shepherd ~
How could I forget?*

*The Lord is my shepherd ~
Then why should I fret?*

My Service

Lou S. Davidson   © 1956

I cannot go to foreign lands
To spread the Gospel there
I cannot give much of my time
My wee ones need my care.

But I can give accordingly
As He has given me
And I can pray for those who go
And write them faithfully.

I can raise our children for Him
According to His Word,
Invite my neighbors in for tea
And tell them of the Lord.

I can teach the little children,
Give out tracts and witness, too.
The many things that God has for
The untalented to do.

Lord, help me not to yearn to do
The bigger jobs for Thee,
But help me do the small one *well*
That you've assigned to me.

New Verse For Child's Prayer

Lou S. Davidson   © 1962

Now I lay me down to sleep
I'll not fear, for thou wilt keep!
If today, in work or play
I have sinned one sin, I pray
Thou wilt forgive and wash away
And keep me safe till break of day.
In Jesus's name, I pray
Amen.

Of Smiles and Tears

By Lou S. Davidson   © 1996

It's sad to see a smile
Driven away by a tear!
Or to see peace and calm
So overtaken by fear.

But one sight I love to see—
When the heart is so outdone
With a joy that is so deep
Both tears and smiles are one!

(Written on remembering the reaction of one I prayed with to ask Jesus into her heart!)

After reading a portion of scripture ending in Matthew 17:27, I thought of all the diverse ways and unexpected means God uses to accomplish His purpose.

Oh, Lord, Use Even Me

By Lou S. Davidson   © 1963

Out of the mouth of a fish
A piece of money was found.
Out of the side of a rock
Cold water did abound.
Out of the sky up above
Choice food fell to the ground.
Oh, Lord, use even me.

Out of an old empty pot
The soil still freely flowed.
Out of a man's withered hand
Was strength again bestowed.
Out of a dark midnight sky
A fiery pillar glowed.
Oh, Lord, use even me.

Out of a dead wooden rod
The tiny buds unfurled.
Out of the letters from Paul
Came sermons to the world.
Out of a young man's sling
That well-aimed stone was hurled.
Oh, Lord, use even me.

One Wish

By Lou S. Davidson   © 1956

If I could have one wish come true,
I would wish for perfect *peace*.
Peace from worry, and peace from fear
Peace that would never, ever cease!

My second wish would be for *joy*
Overflowing, full, sublime,
A joy that would know no ending,
Would not fade nor dim with time.

If I could have a third come true
I would wish for *love* undying;
Love so deep, so great, so boundless
Love so true and satisfying.

Since I've taken Christ as Savior,
His Spirit is with me too.
Abiding in Him in every way
He made my wishes come true.

He has forgiven all my sins
Gives me peace and joy and love
Answers my prayers and grants me fruit
And waits for me above!

Peace At Last

By Lou S. Davidson

I longed for a peace
That would never cease
A friend who would never fail.
I longed for joy
Without alloy.
I searched, but to no avail!

I longed for someone to love me
And someone to love in return.
I longed to be free from the agony
Of my sin with its hidden burn.
Now I sing of the day
Jesus came my way
And I asked Him into my heart.
Now He lives and reigns within me
And He will never depart!

Start A New Day

Lou S. Davidson © *1995*

Lord, take away my cares
I cast them all on thee.
Take me from Satan's grasp
And set me wholly free.

Take every evil thought
Before it comes to mind
Replace it with thy Word
Some new thing I might find.

Let love, joy, peace, and good
(Fruit of thy Spirit, Lord)
Make every daily task
Work out with one accord.

While waiting in the line for the teller to cash my check, I thought about using the time for praying.

I'm so happy we do not have to stand in line when we have needs in our lives, and we know God can listen no matter when or where we are. Thinking along these lines, I came up with this little rhyme.

The Banker

Lou S. Davidson   © 1994

I bend my knee and bow my head
And send a check of prayer,
Signed by faith, the Holy Spirit
Takes it winging through the air!

He takes it to the teller there
Who opened my account
When He died on Calvary
It's an unlimited amount.

He unlocks the safe of heaven
And from His riches there
Finds my sins are all confessed
And sends the answer to my prayer!

The World Gets In My Way

Lou S. Davidson   © 1956

I promised myself that I would pray
Morning, noon, and night each day.
But the day went by, and I'm sad to say
The things of the world got in my way!

I heard Him say, "There's much to do.
This small task I'll give to you."
But I didn't take time to see it through
There were worldly tasks to begin anew.

The devil's subtle, and I'm so weak!
And though for blessings I would seek,
Each time I listen for my Lord to speak
The world's temptation is at its peak!

And so I pray, "Lord, hear my plea.
If you can use someone like me,
Then make the devil and the world to flee
And let my heart seek only *thee*."

To Know Thy Will

By Lou S. Davidson   © 1963

I'm only a sinner Jesus loved.
His death gave me life anew.
He purchased my soul at Calvary.
Lord, what would you have me do?

Only to know thy perfect will,
That I might not go astray.
I would not lag in unbelief
Nor too swiftly lead the way.

Oh, to discern thy Spirit, Lord.
I want to be truly thine;
But Satan works so cunningly
To make his will be mine.

So make the pathway plain, Lord.
Close every door but one.
Make my path so plain, Lord,
That only thy will be done.

To My Missionaries

By Lou S. Davidson   © 1994

*I didn't pray for you today,
As I usually do,
For my prayer was interrupted
Before it was half through!
And all day long, I tried my best
To go back and start anew
But one thing led to another
'til the day, at last, was through!
Now in the quiet, even time
I spend with my Lord in prayer.
He assures me that He knew my heart
And had kept you in His care!*

Wait And Pray

Lou S. Davidson   © 1978

I bought a little golden ring
I wanted for my hand
He said it was the very thing
His gift for me had planned.

I had a monetary need
To borrow I was driven
Then I was told, "If I had known,
The money I'd have given."

Oh, when shall I just wait and pray
That joy might double be
Joy from receiving that I need
For Him who giveth me.

Welcome To God's House

Lou S. Davidson   © 2006

Welcome to my home today.
I'm glad that you are here.
I know you came to sing and pray
And overcome each fear.

Your sins are all forgiven
The moment they're confessed.
Since you had Jesus in your heart
You are truly blessed!

Love of God

Testimony and Service

A New Road From An Old Refrain

Lou S. Davidson   © 1977

There's a new road out my window
That I've never traveled before
    It's shadowed o'er by a mighty oak
    And gold leaves line its floor.
And as it winds along its way
It beckons. "Come along"
    I realize my blinded eyes
    Were opened by a song.

It was just a childhood melody
That seemed to flood my heart
    And the words still in my memory
    Escaped me at the start
But the words, joined with the melody,
Returned to me again
    First a phrase and then another—
    I sang that old refrain:

        "I'll go where you want me to *go*, dear Lord,
            O'er mountain or land or sea.
        I'll do what you want me to *do*, dear Lord,
            I'll be what you want me to *be*."

And now I sing, not just a song
    But a solemn prayerful vow
For whatever road He has for me,
    I'm ready to travel now.
I'm ready to leave the world's delights.
    Oh, that I had done it back then
When first I sang that old refrain
    As now, I sing it again.

        "And if, by a still small voice He calls,
            To paths I do not know
        I'll whisper, dear Lord, with your hand in mine,
            I'll go where you want me to go."

God's Challenge

Lou S. Davidson   © 1963

Lou S. Davidson   Ada P. Soubirou
   (Lyrics)   (Music)

If you love Christ as Savior,
If you're in His Command,
Oh! will you meet the challenge,
Our lives are in your hand.

Chorus:

Lead us, train us,
With love constrain us
Guide us as we should go.
Teach us, mold us,
So all who behold us
The love of Christ shall know.

    Verse II
We know Him as our Savior,
But we must grow in grace
We're thirsty for much knowledge
Ere we shall see His face.

    Verse III
We are the future leaders
But now we look to you
To fit us for His service
That we might serve Him too.

(Written for the theme song at our church's missionary conference)

God's Challenge

used by permission

LOU S. DAVIDSON   ADA P. SOUBIROU

1. If you love Christ as Sav-iour; If you're in His Com-mand;
2. We know Him as our Sav-iour, But we must grow in grace.
3. We are the fu-ture lead-ers, But now we look to You

Oh! will you meet the Chal-lenge? Our lives are in Your hand.
We're thir-sty for much know-ledge Ere we shall see His face.
To fit us for His Serv-ice That we might serve Him too.

Chorus

Lead us, train us; With love con-strain us, Guide us as we should

Teach us, mold us, So all who be-hold us, The love know.

Finish the Job

Lou S. Davidson   © 1957

Whenever the cares of the present day
     Insist on taking first place
Look up to the cross where Jesus died
     Look up to His tender face.
Instead of the cross, think of the crown
     Step into a more rapid pace,
Ere the day has gone,
     You'll finish the job,
     Girded and led by His grace.

Temptation is always Satan's tool
     There when you least expect it
Remember, you're doing work for the Lord
     He's sure to help you reject it.

Follow Jesus closely, trusting Him
     He'll lend to you His power
To keep you each moment, and lend His peace
     Till you reach that final hour!

His Servants

Lou S. Davidson   © 1994

The days are long and the job's undone—
It seems there's always another one!
No loving praise for what you do—
Only . . . "Here's another job for you!"

But we're not in it for the week-end pay
And we don't mind the long-houred day.
We just work through the tempest wild
Just to hear Him say, "Well done, my child!"

Matthew 25:21 says, "Enter thou into the joy of Thy Lord."

Many hours were the norm for our daughter Joy and her husband, Billy, as they managed a community kitchen, men's and women's shelters, and thrift store for a North Georgia-based ministry. On one of our visits, we observed the behind-the-scenes work and effort it took, far exceeding a regular daily shift, and our hearts were encouraged as we knew their true reward would be one day in heaven.

Just Imagine

Lou S. Davidson © *1999*

Just imagine what the Lord could do
With a guy like you
Or a gal like you!

Just imagine what the Lord could do
If you let Him do
What He wants to do

Just imagine what the Lord could do
If you let Him work with you!

Lord, Lead Me Today

Lou S. Davidson   © 2007

Lord, lead me to a soul today
That I may tell of thee,
And of thy power to save
As thou hast done for me.

Lord, lead me to a soul today
Who wanders deep in sin,
That he may open up his heart
In faith and let thee in.

Lord, lead me to a soul today
Who loves thee more than I,
That I may too be challenged
Before the day goes by.

To search my heart's deep secrets
And feed upon thy Word.
Then send me forth to take it
To souls who've never heard.

    When a person does not learn of Jesus Christ until something terrible happens in their lives, it makes them fervently want to give the Good News to others who have never heard or who have never had anyone help them to pray and ask Jesus into their heart.
    I was the first one in my family to be saved, and that was long after I had spent many years in Sunday school and church. Over many years, I had the joy of seeing all of my family come to the Lord. Momma asked Jesus into her heart under the clothesline while hanging out the wash. Daddy accepted the Lord after a Billy Graham TV broadcast. Two sisters began their relationship with the Lord in our home, and a brother prayed over the telephone.
    It took a catastrophic event in my life to make me search for answers. My personal circumstances have made me want to give the Good News to anyone that will listen and to go a step further to help them pray. Many opportunities are there if we're willing to look for them.

On Giving

Lou S. Davidson © 1994

Three hundred and thirty heard the need
      A worthy cause they all agreed
If each would give 't would be so nice
      And thirty of them made a sacrifice.

The others said, "I really do care—
      But just a dollar is all I could spare
With so many others on the list
      I'm sure my dollar won't be missed!"

The pastor said, "It is really nice
      That some have made such a sacrifice,
I'm very sad, but I must report
      We were just three hundred dollars short!"

    How often do we think our "little bit" is insignificant? We forget great ability of making much out of little and how everyone's little makes much together!

On Witnessing

Lou S. Davidson   © 1994

I had a dream the other night
It woke me up with quite a fright!
It seems I met the Lord of Love
But it was down here, not up above!

He asked me why I was so cruel
To so many others as a rule.
I did not tell them of His love
Or how they, too, could rise above.

I kept my faith to myself, He said.
But I should pass it on instead,
That others could know Him as I do
And have His love and forgiveness too.

"I'm sorry," I said. "But I'm shy you know."
He said, "Just tell them everywhere you go.
Tell them so they can know me too!
Don't care about what they think of *you*!"

I see so many people come and go. I wish I could tell each one about the Lord and how much joy and peace He can give them. Sometimes I begin a conversation by asking them where they go to church for an icebreaker, but it seems that I still feel that I should have tried harder to share my faith.

I had taken time to rest and tried not to fall asleep. However, I must have dozed off because all at once, I had the urge to write this poem. Before I could get up and get to the table, the first verse was already flowing out. As fast as I could write the words, they came to my mind.

How many times do we say, "Naah, I'm not going to say anything. They'll think I'm some kind of fanatic or something." So we just let them go on their way. This thought prompted the last line of this poem.

Our Mighty God

By Lou S. Davidson © 1979

"I rest my foot upon the earth
      And heaven is my throne
Each star, I've named and anchored
      For each one is my own."
Creation is my doing
      According to my own plan;
What need have I for anything?
      What need have I for man?

Still it pleased the Lord to bruise Him
      Our iniquities did Him in;
He poured His life out unto death
      To take away our sin.
Even a very little child
      Who in his heart believes
Can know joy and peace within
      When Jesus he receives.

He calls, the Lord of creation
      Is calling even you.
Will you answer, believe, and serve,
      Go where He tells you to?
Go and serve unselfishly
      In the name of the Lord
For if you do, He tells us,
      "Ye shall not lose your reward."

Sow to Reap

Lou S. Davidson   © 1966

"Blessed are your eyes for they see"*
You have received the seed in good ground
Be not deceived by wealth and care
Let not persecution bring fear
That abundance of fruit may abound.

So go, therefore, sow precious seed
Where the enemy soweth tares
Ere the angels shall sever the two.
The field is the world sore in need,
And souls slip away unawares
Ask the master just what you should do

How shall they hear the holy Word
To cancel traditions' decay?
How shall they preach except they be sent?
Pray therefore the Lord of the harvest
That He speak to your heart today
Till you "lengthen the cords"† of your tent.

---

*   Matthew 13:16
†   Isaiah 54:2

The Death of His Saints

Lou S. Davidson   © 1956

"Precious in the sight of the Lord
Is the death of His saints."*
We know,
And surely we can understand
Why God's Word tells us so.

He has redeemed me from my sin
He paid the price on Calvary.
And through this gift, I'll enter in
Where He's prepared a place for me.

His will and work I'll strive to do.
A pilgrim in this land, I roam
And look on death as precious too
Until He bids me to come home.

Today Mother Davidson left on the
8:20 angel for heaven, April 16, 1956.

---

* Psalm 116:15

To Do or Not To Do

Lou S. Davidson   © 1965

He looked at the list of the things to be done
And the problems remaining unsolved
"I know I should,
and I know I could,
But I don't want to get involved!"

He wasn't content with all that was spent
Or the way events revolved
He gave up in vain,
for he wouldn't complain,
For fear of getting involved!

Use Me, Lord

Lou S. Davidson   © 2000

I don't want to move a mountain
Or divide a rolling sea
But just want to share the faith
That you have given me.

Faith to believe your promises
Not just for reaching heaven,
But walking with thee every day
Not just one out of seven.

Faith to ask for your healing power
For those who need it so
A means of bringing them to thee
Your saving grace to know.

So I pray for faith and knowledge
Your will to do today
Oh, let me bring lost souls to thee
As I go on my way.

What Would You Have Me To Do, Lord?

Lou S. Davidson   © 1961

What would you have me to do, Lord—
What would you have me to do?
You gave your all on Calvary.
Sought, redeemed, and purchased me
Now that you have set me free,
What would you have me to do?

What would you have me to give, Lord—
What would you have me to give?
I have given thee my heart
But I know that's just a start.
Now I want to do my part.
What would you have me to give?

Where would you have me to go, Lord—
Where would you have me to go?
I see the harvest is white.
Oh, how they need the Light.
Lord, speak to my heart tonight.
Where would you have me to go?

Love of God

Poems of Hope and Encouragement

A Foolish Choice

Lou S. Davidson   © 1993

I cleaned out the box under the bed.
All the papers were very old.
What a disappointment to say the least!
I had hoped for silver or gold!

One of them was fifteen years of age,
He wrote it with an old ink pen.
I saw my name there with all the rest
But I was just a young child then.

So I burnt them, but I kept the box
"With my little trinkets I'll fill."
I burnt the treasure but kept the trash,
For I had burnt up father's will!

Young people, beware of your actions!
Make choices your parents instill,
Or you may regret your choices in life
If you don't comprehend God's will!

Daydreams

Lou S. Davidson   © 1998

We dream at night
    But we have no say
Of the thoughts that come
    Or how long they stay.

But every day
    With an open mind
We can plan the future,
    And seek and find.

So thank the Lord
    For your blessings now.
Let Him show the way.
    Let Him tell you how!

There are no limits
    If you do your part.
He'll make things happen
    If He's in your heart!

Friday Morning

Lou S. Davidson © 1995

I was depressed, alone, and downhearted,
      Each wrong I had done washed over my soul
The chores of the day like mountains to climb
      I dreaded my lot—my life as a whole!

But then I thanked God for a good breakfast
      And asked Him to bless and nourish me;
To feed my soul with the Bread of Life
      Then it seemed as though He had set me free.

Then while reading my daily devotions
      Like balloons popping, one by one
Each bit of turmoil, trouble, and care,
      Was now washed away, over and done!

As I thought of the day still before me
      To plan each hour just as I please
To figure each task and commitment
      My schedule, *my* work, and *my* ease!

So I thanked God for spending time with me
      The light of His Spirit within my heart—
The way He helped me through His Word
      To begin this day on a happy start!

God Knows

Lou S. Davidson

I'm too tired to trust and too tired to pray
Said one as the overtaxed strength gave way.
The one conscious thought my mind possessed,
Is, *Oh, could I just drop it all and rest?*

Will God forgive one, do you suppose,
If I go right to sleep as a baby goes,
Without an asking if I may,
Without ever trying to trust and pray?

Will God forgive you? Why think, dear heart,
When language to you was an unknown art,
Did a mother deny you needed rest,
Or refuse to pillow your head on her breast?

Did she let you want when you could not ask?
Did she set her child on unequal task,
Or did she cradle you in her arms,
And then guard your slumber against alarms?

Ah, how quick was her mother-love to see,
The unconscious yearnings of infancy.
When you've grown too tired to trust and pray,
When overwrought nature has quite given way,

Then just drop it all and give up the rest
As you used to do on your mother's breast.
He knows all about it, the dear Lord knows,
So just go to sleep as a baby goes.

Without even asking if you may
God knows when His child is too tired to pray.
He judges not solely by uttered prayer.
He knows when the yearnings of love are there.

He knows you do pray, He knows you do trust,
And He knows, too, the limits of poor weak dust.
Oh, the wonderful sympathy of Christ,
For His chosen ones in that midnight tryst,

When He bade them sleep and take their rest,
While on Him the guilt of the whole world pressed.
You've given your life up to Him to keep,
Then don't be afraid to go right to sleep!

I Have Seen the Christ

Lou S. Davidson © 1963

I have seen the Christ! "Nay," you say.
Oh yes, I've seen Him many times today:

I saw Him in a teacher's love as she taught a little child,
I saw Him in my daughter's eyes as she looked at me and smiled.
I saw Him in my beloved as he bowed his head to pray;
I saw Him in a widow's life as she leans on Him each day.
In the beauty all around me, their designer is portrayed
In every tree and flower fair He so perfectly has made.

I have heard Him speak! Honestly!
Today, quite clearly, He spoke to me:

Through love in the voice of a friend o'er cables miles long,
In the tenderness of wisdom from one so big and strong.
The joy in children as they sang their Savior to acclaim.
In the precious sound of "Mama" when it becomes my name.
Through the pages of the scriptures though penned so long ago,
And in my prayers, He speaks to me the things He'd have me know.

I Need Another Miracle

Lou S. Davidson   © 1994

Lord, I could not know such peace now
      Had you not tried me in the past
For I know your love and mercy
      When all my care on thee is cast.

I go back into memory
      To all the times I called to you
You answered prayers by doing things
      That were impossible to do.

"There is nothing too hard for me"
      I have read in your written Word
To think you cannot handle this
      Would be really quite absurd.

So I'll rejoice in gratitude
      Not asking if or when or how
But trusting that my "mustard seed"
      Can move this mountain for me now.

> Matthew 17:20 says, "If ye have faith as a grain of
> mustard seed, ye shall say unto this mountain,
> Remove hence to yonder place and it shall remove."

Jesus Can

Lou S. Davidson © *1965*

A mile isn't far if you're happy
The day isn't long if you're gay,
The night isn't dark if you're not alone
When you sing no sorrow can stay.

Only Jesus can make you happy
Only Jesus can show you the way.
He'll impart a song to your heart,
So won't you trust Him today?

Jesus Said It

Lou S. Davidson © *1977*

Jesus said it,
I believe it,
And that settles it!

Jesus said it,
I believe it,
And that settles it!

I don't understand
Everything I've heard
But I know it's true
If it's in God's Word

Jesus said it,
I believe it,
And that settles it!

Not Go To Church?

Lou S. Davidson   © 3/30/93

Not go to church? Would you take away
The joy of meeting God in His house on His day?
Not go to pray?

Not go to church? And then miss the sound
Of voices blending full with music all around
With joy abound?

Not go to church? Where else can you find
A beginning that is new—the past is left behind
Then peace of mind?

Not go to church? To thank the One who died
There on the cruel cross for your sin crucified
Now justified?

Not go to church? I pray that I shall be
Grateful to all those who provided church for me.
Just come and see!

On Fasting

Lou S. Davidson   © 1996

Dear Lord,

>I come to thee in prayer this hour.
>Lord, fill me by thy gracious power
>With nourishment that's truly thine.
>Let thy radiant Spirit shine!
>
>What dainty bit or frozen treat
>Could satisfy or be more sweet?
>As I forfeit the scheduled meal
>Your loving touch I gently feel.
>
>With time unhurried and alone,
>My praise and needs are all made known.
>My sins confessed, thy grace I know.
>And faith renewed, I rise to go
>With heartfelt joy to conquer strife.
>You've fed me with the Bread of Life!

It was suggested at church that we skip one meal on Wednesdays and fast and pray for that hour instead. On Wednesday morning, I went to the ladies' bible study and prayer meeting at Jean's home and came away fully blessed with her good in-depth teaching and the circle of fervent prayers. It was shortly after noon, so I decided that I would use my six o'clock hour for my time for prayer and fasting.

About five forty-five, I decided to fast and pray for an hour then go to prayer meeting at seven. I started with prayer then began reading the first chapter of Esther. Before I knew it, I had finished that book! I prayed again, praising God for the privilege, thanking Him for His grace, compassion, and care. I looked up at the clock! Prayer meeting had already begun! I don't think I ever did say "amen." As I just thought of that experience, I felt I should just take the time to put it into words. It came out in *rhyme*!

On Smoking

Lou S. Davidson © 1994

"Don't start!" Dad said.
Mom said it too!
But a young teen does
What other teens do!

"I'll quit when I'm ready,
I know that I will,
But until that time
I'll continue still!"

"I love you," she said
"But marry you? *No!*
You know that habit
Would have to go!"

"Then, I'll quit," he said
And he meant it too.
"And as of right now
You can call it 'through'!"

In an hour, he knew
That it was too late
That stinking habit
Had sealed his fate!

Years later, he said,
"I'll conquer it yet!"
But he's still *under control*
Of a cigarette!

    It takes a stronger person to *resist temptation*, than to take a *dare*.

Our busy schedules, sometimes too full of duties and responsibilities for daily living, may distract us from a direction God wants us to go. I came up with the idea that if we "got paid" at the end of each day from the Lord—would we be more careful with how we spent our time?

Payday

Lou S. Davidson   © 1994

If we had to line up at the end of each day
As workers do to receive their pay
I wonder what God would have to say
Of the time that we had whiled away!

If we had to answer to God each night
For what we'd done wrong, or if we did right,
We might stand there in a terrible fright
If we had not served with all our might!

So today whatever I say or do,
Dear God, I'll do it as unto you.
And at the close of this tiring day
All I want is to hear you say

"Well done, thou good and faithful servant;
Thou hast been faithful over a few things,
I will make thee ruler over many things:
Enter thou into the joy of thy Lord" (Mt 25:21).

After Dr. Crowder's Sunday's message on *salt* from Matthew 5, these thoughts kept running around in my mind until I finally sat down and wrote them into a poem.

Reclaiming Your Power

Lou S. Davidson   © 1983

Have you lost your savor?
Are you trodden underfoot of man?
Are you no longer the "salt of the earth"*
Because you're not following God's plan?

Have you lost your candle?
Is there a bushel hiding its glow?
Are your works all selfish and worthless deeds
And not the kind God's mercy would show?

Go to the Lord in prayer,
Humbly confessing to Him your sin.
Remember He died on the cross for you
He'll renew a "right spirit" within.

Just trust and rest in His Word
Read His promises over once more
Claim the *victory* and forget the past
You'll do better than ever before!

"If we confess our sin, He is faithful and just to forgive us our sin and to cleanse us from all unrighteousness" (1 John 1:9).

"Ye are the salt of the earth" (Matthew 5:13a)

Rise to Glory

Lou S. Davidson   © *1994*

Ill with a fever and cough, I lay
There on the sofa at close of day;
But Daddy was close, his watch to keep
And soon I fell into peaceful sleep.

Then in his arms, and with loving care
He carried me up each rising stair
I never knew he had changed my place
Till I felt the sunshine on my face.

Completely well, the fever was gone!
And I marveled at the bright new morn.
I think that's how it's going to be
When I awake—in heaven—with thee!

Psalm 17:15 says, "I shall be satisfied, when I awake,
with thy likeness."

Telling the Way

Lou S. Davidson   © 1975

It could be today that my Lord would say,
"Come up hither," I know
If it were today that He called me away
Would I be ready to go?

Could I know and know for sure
That my loved ones would follow me there?
And my neighbors ~ would they honestly say
That I had showed them the Way?

When my friends hear you say the phrase
"With Him all my days"
Will they say that I shared Him with them?
Or will this glory for me when they finally see
Will it only help to condemn?

Lord, help me today to do and to say,
All that I should for you.
I need your courage, your strength, and your help
For the job that you gave me to do.

That when that day comes, and it could be today,
That all who have known me might say—

"She told me of Jesus, the Savior of man,
And tried to show me the way

"And I'm happy for her and I know, oh so well,
She's with her Savior today."

Ten Minutes

Lou S. Davidson   © 1973

Ten minutes in the morning
To read your Bible and pray.
Ten minutes in the morning
Can make or break your day.

Read what God would say to you
And give your thanks to Him,
Confess your unkind words and thoughts
Don't let your lamp grow dim ~

That ten minutes in the morning
At night will make you say
"Thank you, God, for your faithfulness,
I had a happy day!"

The Ideal Christian

Lou S. Davidson   © 1949

Did you ever ask your Father
What He would have you be?
Turn to First Thessalonians
And in chapter 1, you'll see:

Paul wrote this great epistle
That folks like you and me
May know what an ideal Christian
In God's sight ought to be:

First we must have heard God's Word
And of Jesus Christ, His Son,
Who died on Calvary's cross for us
When victory over sin was won.

When our hearts are filled with truths,
And we have confessed our sin
We open up our hearts with joy
And our Savior enters in.

Then we find that we are born again
That all things now are new
And we turn our eyes on Jesus
And try His will to do.

We realize our blessings more
As we live in Christ each day.
And we testify to others
As we go along life's way.

We serve a *living* Savior!
And in triumph or in strife
We remember we're examples
So we live a holy life.

We have that pure contentment
That only Christians know
And we know He hears our prayers
When to the throne of grace we go.

Now we await His coming, and we'll meet Him in the air
When He'll take us home to heaven
And we meet our Father there.

>Lou S. Davidson
>March 22, 1949

(Written after Dr. Woodbridge's teaching on chapter 1 of 1 Thessalonians)

The Old Letter

Lou S. Davidson   © 1994

I found an old letter he'd written.
It was to someone I never knew.
He talked of things I had never heard
Yet I knew that each word was true.

I thought of the joy I was knowing
Though some pages were very dim,
Just to know that it was his writing,
Filled me with love thoughts of him.

Now each time I read the old prophets,
And saints who lived so long ago,
I find a peace and a joy within
Because it's the *author* I know.

One day as I was reading the book of Ezekiel, I had the thought, *So, what's in it for me?* Then I realized that it didn't matter what the words were, it was *God's Word* I was reading! Although it might seem irrelevant to know about Ezekiel's times today, I still had a feeling of being close to God as I read it.

I thought of when I had been cleaning out some old papers after Kenny's dad went to be with the Lord. As I read through some letters, I could recognize who had written them. Even though I did not know the people the letters involved, I still had known *him*. I could recognize his manner of speaking, his kindness, and his keen business sense. I was amazed at how close he seemed as I read them.

So now when I read the Old Testament, I read it looking for God's kindness and faithfulness, love, and all of His other attributes. It's easy to find them once you recognize the author!

The Picture

Lou S. Davidson   © 1953

The picture of my Savior,
Though it hangs for all to see,
As I've gazed upon it through the years
Has grown so dear to me.

For it serves as a reminder
Of His tender love and care
And it disciplines my deepest thoughts
As I see it hanging there.

At times when I am wayward
And let self-will reign awhile,
It seems He frowns! Then I confess
And I think I see Him smile.

A picture of Salman's famous painting of the head of Christ was a special gift to Kenny and to me. It has hung in a place of honor in every home we've lived in for all these years.

While listening to a lady giving her testimony on Dale Evan's television program, I was impressed by a phrase she used. She said of the time before she became a Christian, "I thought there must be more to life than this!"

I remembered how many times I had used that same phrase in my dark past. But never again since the day I asked Jesus to come into my heart. He came in, took away my sin, made me a *child of God* and gave me a new and glorious life, much more to life than I could have imagined!

There Must Be More to Life Than This

Lou S. Davidson   © 1993

Another day, another dollar
Another date, a good-night kiss
Another problem and solution
There must be more to life than this!

Another gain, another trial
Another plan that went amiss
Another dream about tomorrow
There must be more to life than this!

Another sermon, this one taken
To the heart and Christ received!
There's much more to life, I know now,
Since the day I first believed.

Joy and peace through every conflict
A tomorrow of perfect bliss;
For I believe beyond the grave
There *is more* to life than *this*!

Today!

Lou S. Davidson   © 1970

Oh could we turn the hands of time
Back to another day
When our great land was in its prime
And righteousness held sway!

When Sunday was the Lord's Day,
"In God we trust" meant what it said.
United in a common cause
With Christ, the honored head!

Oh no, we cannot turn the tide,
But we can change today,
For Christ the Savior crucified,
Is still the only way!

Then with His resurrection power
With yielded hearts in prayer.
We win the hearts of those next door
Thus reach men everywhere!

Walk By Faith

Lou S. Davidson   © 1973

I can walk with Him in glory here
On earth from day to day.
I can know the joy and peace
Now of His love.
I can feel Him ever present
Though sorrows come my way
'Til He comes to take me (With Him up above.)

Oh, it's joy and peace and happiness
When you're walking in His love.
It's joy to walk by faith alone.
So show forth this joy
And happiness;
Then pass it on with love
To someone who has never known.

What God Can Do

Lou S. Davidson   © 1995

God wrote the Ten Commandments
      With His finger on the stone
That Moses had prepared for Him
      His will to be made known!

God stacked the Jordan's waters high
      That Elisha might pass through
When He saw his faith in action,
      And He'll do the same for you.

So if you want to serve the Lord
      And serve with all your might
There's nothing God won't do for you
      If He thinks that it is *right*.

You Didn't Ask

Lou S. Davidson   © 1995

"You complained about the problem
You complained about the task
I longed to work a miracle
But, my dear, you didn't ask!"

"The money that would meet the need
Seemed such a great amount
So you only asked for part of it
But I would have met the count."

"The very life of someone dear
Would take a miracle indeed!
Instead you prayed for comfort
For the loved ones in their need."

"There is nothing too hard for *me*,
No insurmountable a task—
But if I do not work the work
Was it because you didn't ask?"

My Darling Earl.

Beloved Husband
Earl Smythe

November 17, 1914
to June 7, 1944

Love and Loneliness

Poems of Earl

The White Gown

Lou S. Davidson   © 3/1/56

A drifting, billowy, cloud of white
The gown I wore that magic night
He held me tight and kissed me then
He said, "We must do this again."

The next year, we'd repeat the night
I planned again a gown of white
But screeching brakes as cars collide
Stole my love in an ambulance ride.

But faith was strong and love was true
And his eyes and bones were good as new
I'd stop my work, we'd settle down
And celebrate! (A new white gown).

The yards and yards of white Moire
Folds and tucks as I sewed away.
Then at last! A vision fulfilled
But never worn, that day he was killed.

That magic night was meant to be
Not repeated—but a memory;
And though my world came crashing down
We'll meet again—in a snow-white gown.*

Note: A flaming B-24 was to blame, but the Lord was gracious and gave me another husband for forty-three wonderful years. I laughed when the person planning the second wedding said that since I had been married before I could not have a *white* gown. I made a blue one.

---

*   Revelation 19:8

I Think Of You

Lou M. Smythe   © 12/3/46

To Earl:

When I'm alone like this at night,
Or when I walk with the moon in sight,
When the music's low and I dim the light,
    Somehow—I think of you.

When a new day has just begun
Or I sneeze from the glaring noonday sun
Or wandering home—the day's work done
    I find—I think of you.

I hear a song that someone sings
A telephone—with two short rings
Arranging flowers someone brings
    And then—I think of you.

What do I think when I think of you?
An answer to this I sought
It's an indescribable feeling inside
    That couldn't be called a "thought."

    This poem is another that was a result of my hurting, lonely heart struggling to bear my loss. I had moved to Miami Beach, Florida, and at this time, it seemed that there would never be another happy moment in my life. So often, my only consolation was to get it out into the form of a poem. Had I been able to see just around the corner, I would have been elated at the events and happenings heading my way, but at the present, I was forlorn and sorely missing my dear departed husband.

The Story Behind "OUR MONTHIVERSARY"

I had joined the WAVES after Earl's unexpected death. I was stationed in the Navy Department in Washington DC and living in barracks in Arlington, Virginia. My brother Delmar C. Merritt, Jr. was two years older than I and was also in the service and away from his family. We shared our lonely moments by APO mail.

This poem, dated June 7, 1945, was sent to him somewhere at sea on a destroyer escort in the Pacific. About forty-four years later at his funeral, a much discolored, folded piece of paper with the creases worn through was handed to me. Alice, his dear wife, said, "This was in Del's wallet all these years. I thought you'd like to have it back."

The poem had been typed, but handwritten at the top was "DEL, Here's something that ran thru my mind, I jotted it down. What do you think of it?"

EARL'S KAYAK: 1939

Our Monthiversary

Lou S. Davidson   © 1945

Our "Monthiversary"—a crazy name
But we were playing a grand new game!
I was so proud to hear him say,
"This is my wife—one month today!"

Then happiness reigned and joy supreme
Fulfilled each plan, each childhood dream.
I knew he loved me more than words could say,
And I thrilled when he said, "A year today."

We knew what it meant to laugh and sing
And to enjoy the peace that faith can bring
When he lay so still—so close to death
"Three years today!" He gasped for breath.

But God was good and He let him stay
He grew strong again and we stole away
To explore new fields we had never known
And we liked it there—it became our home.

There was a boat he'd built—a river nearby
And there, one night, 'neath a darkening sky
On an island, I thrilled to his passionate kiss—
"Four years today—and it's still like this!"

But he was young and strong at will
And aircraft offered a greater thrill.
He loved his work—and flying was fun
And it wouldn't be long till the war was won.

The days went fast and as they passed
Each one was greater than the last
And our hearts were high as he said that day,
"You've been my wife five years today."

Another year, though the world was at war,
Our love was stronger than ever before.
We had proved our worth and faith, and soon
"'Twould be six years since our honeymoon."

And now my world is dark with pain
As I visualize the flaming plane
I love him more than I can say
Though I'm a *widow*—one year today.

        In memory of my beloved hubby, Earl

        June 7, 1945

My *Little Engagement Bunny*

Lou S. Davidson   ©1938

*You know, my dear, 'tis the strangest thing
But 'neath my pillow—all made of string
Is a little guy I call your name
And I'm so happy since he came!*

*He holds me tight through the lonely hours
And walks with me through paths of flowers,
And all night long he guides my way
Through a heavenly dreamland while you're away.*

*And all the horrors that filled my dreams
And wakened me with my own screams
He's turned to dreams of happiness
And calms my fears with his tender kiss.*

*Now every night I kneel to pray
That he will never go away
Until my fondest dream comes true
When I awake to find him—you!*

This poem was written in 1938. I was engaged to Earl Smythe. On our date, he brought me the little bunny. Because of my delight and then writing the poem to mark the occasion, Earl continued to add to the collection each week on payday. Each little critter was different, and the last one was a huge teddy bear!

Would You?

Lou S. Davidson   © 1937

Would you make me over
      Darling, if you might?
Would you mold me to a plan
      Patterned prim and right?
Would you mute my laughter
      And curb my racing tongue?
Would you have me older
      Or would you have me young?

Would you make me over
      Every little part,
Demanding certain changes
      In soul and mind and heart
Conforming to your blueprints
      And mental diagram?
Or, darling, will you love me
      Simply as I am?

              Lou

A Prayer

Lou S. Davidson   © October 13, 1938

Oh, Father, now I turn to thee
And pray that I may someday be
Just what Earl would want me to
And do the things he'd have me do;

Give me strength and self-control
To help me reach that heavenly goal
That I am ever striving for—
His love—nothing more.

Hide my aching want for him
Thus keep the lamp from growing dim
And make him want me more and more
With all the love his heart can store!

Bless him for all his decency
Pour a bit more pride in me
Make me indifferent to his caress
And still not make me love him less.
                    Amen

Our Fifth Anniversary

Lou S. Davidson © June 25, 1943

Dear Earl:

    Just eighteen hundred and twenty-five days ago,
I married you—and little did I know
    That it would mean such happiness and bliss
Nor by this time, that I'd still feel like this

    The little things you've done along the way
Your smile, your laugh, the crazy things you say!
    The way you understand no matter what I do,
The thrill I get whenever I'm with you

    Your loving care that always follows me
And thoughts of future joys that are still to be,
    So many things, things I just can't say
You know, little things I have tucked away.

    For every minute of the last five years,
The love—and fun—and even the tears;
    I love you, dear, I will all my life!
Darling, I'm proud to be your *wife*!

    With all my love forever,

        Lou

    When I wrote this poem to Earl, I had no idea that we had less than a year left to be together.

    We left Lambertville and moved to Pennsylvania. He got work at an air base there. When the war started, he tried to join the navy but could not because of his job in an "essential" industry. I got a good job in the plant department of the telephone company. We were so happy!

When all of my lady friends were lamenting the absence of their husbands who had all been called to war, I was the lucky one with my husband here at home.

However, when bombers had completed fifty missions over Germany, they were brought back here to be serviced. One day when Earl and a team of men went on a routine check flight, something went wrong. It crashed. I was a widow.

About Earl

Lou S. Davidson   © 1995

Would he have done a painting
    That would have brought him fame?
Or would one of the sports be
    Fulfillment of his aim?

Would he have gone to college
    To make teaching his career?
Or have sailed a giant ship
    To ports both far and near?

Would the Lord have given us
    A child or two to raise
And a home high on a hill
    Where all the cows could graze?

Whatever fame or fortune
    I'm sure it is a fact
Nothing ever could surpass
    His last unselfish act.

    When the men came to tell me of the crash of the B-24, one said, "This may help you to feel better about this.

    "Only one man was saved. He had two children. When we picked him up, he said, 'Earl was the only one who took a parachute. He took it off and put it on me and said, "You have to raise those kids," and kicked me out of the plane.'"

    All of the others perished in the flames and were scattered with the parts of the plane over the open fields. When I asked what "BBR" on the death certificate meant, I was told it meant "burnt beyond recognition."

    We had a closed-casket funeral, so I still remember him as the same handsome, loving husband he was for six wonderful years.

    I often wonder about those children.

After having been happily married for six years and thinking of the many songs we sang and the many nights we went either to New York or Willow Grove to dance to the big bands and hear the soloists sing, the thought came to me that so many were songs of heartache and not true love songs.

At that time, I was not the one writing songs or poems—Earl was. He would get his guitar and tell me to go sit across the room from him, then he would play and sing those *old, old,* songs and even wrote one especially for me. "I See a Cottage."

All of these memories would flood my thoughts at times, and it didn't take long to jot down a few thoughts then put them into rhyme.

Since all of my early writings were lost during my transition and as I was now happily married to Ken, this was pulled from memory and typed up in 1949.

No True Love Songs
By Lou M. Smythe

When you were here with me, I used to wonder why
There were no songs of happy folks, such as you and I.

Each love song held a heartache of shattered plans and hearts
Or was just a silly jingle of how a romance starts.

There were no songs of deep true love strengthened by happy years
No songs of trust and tenderness but always sorrow or tears.

Now that you've been called away and I face the world alone
Memories burn within my heart of the love that we have known.

I know now why the song trend is to the aching heart
Not of happy couples, but those who are apart.

For I never thought to put in rhyme, that happiness, it seems
But find that I, like all the rest, now write of shattered dreams.

Still Searching

Lou M. Smythe   © Oct. 14, 1946

To Earl:

    Still searching, looking, grasping, hoping to find
    Someone just like someone left behind
    Each day more and more I understand
    It's searching for diamonds in the sand!

    Were he not so perfect—so flawless, so complete,
    Had he not loved me so—made life so sweet!
    If all my soul were not so wholly his
    I would fail to grieve so long and sad as this!

    Just as our God—omnipotent is He
    A duplicate or substitute can never be.
    And I am never lonesome, nor without His love
    I still feel His tender guidance from above.

    I wrote "Still Searching" when I was in Miami Beach, Florida. I was twenty-six years old at the time this poem was written. Everyone I met was married or had been. I felt the impossibility of finding another husband becoming more real every day. I wanted to belong to someone! I wanted a family! It was a miracle when the Lord brought Ken and I together! How thankful I was then and still am today.

To Earl in Heaven

Lou S. Davidson © 1944

My Darling—

God made you much too perfectly
    To live with others here;
You were too good, too kind, and true
    Your faith was too sincere.

You loved me oh so much, too much
    And kept my love for you
Forever hungry for your touch
    So firm yet gentle too!

Your voice, your song, your daily task
    Your every move and thought
You lived a true religion
    The kind the Savior taught.

God lends each one of us to earth
    For a certain task, and then
When He can say to us, "Well done!"
    He calls us home again.

May the righteousness you taught me
    In such a loving way
Still cling to me and let me be
    More like you were, each day.

That soon my task will be fulfilled
    And while my youth endures
The way you loved me, be brought home,
    My soul placed next to yours.

    Your own,
        Lou

I Found Peace At Last

Lou S. Davidson   © 2007

The flaming B-24 exploded
Then it crashed into the ground
He was probably killed on impact
As the plane was strewn all around.

It was such a terrifying moment
How would I ever forget
BBR—"burnt beyond recognition"
Invades my quiet time yet.

But I'm certain that he is in heaven
For he said, right from the start,
"My dear, you have religion in your head,
But you need Christ in your heart!"

That day in a church on Miami Beach
When I said the "Sinner's Prayer"
I knew then that he had gone to heaven
And that I would meet him there!

But still I had many a nightmare-night
Until my baptism came.
When I came up, I thought it was heaven
Then I knew he escaped that flame!

    I was saved in a Presbyterian church and had been baptized by sprinkling as a baby. However, after I finally was born again, and God gave me Ken Davidson and a new life. Ken and I talked of being baptized by immersion, but we didn't have a baptismal in our Church.

    One day, a dear friend, a wonderful soloist, came to town and stayed at our home. The subject came up, and he stated that he had always felt strange when he sang in a Baptist church, that he had not been baptized that way. So we called our pastor and asked about the possibility of being immersed.

He said that he had an arrangement with the Baptist church if we wanted to do it on a Monday. That next Monday, we were there.

It was a beautiful sanctuary with stained glass windows. I was the first: the handkerchief over my nose and mouth, the pastor's arm behind my shoulders lowering me under the water, then being raised, and *oh,* as I looked out into that beauty, I was sure that I had died and gone to heaven! Oh, what glory! It seemed that I was no longer in my body and I said, "That's what it's like to die! Earl didn't feel those flames!"

I don't know what happened next, but I knew God had given me the peace I needed.

The other day as I was packing to move, I found a box that had not been opened for more than forty-five years. It was full of the newspaper pictures of the flaming plane and some pictures of Earl, the letters concerning his burial, a picture in the paper on the obituary page, the picture of me for my announcement of my engagement to Ken.

Ginni was here helping me to pack and to be with me for Mothers' Day, so we opened the box. There I found a poem in my handwriting, which I wrote on September 29, 1944. He died on June 7. I joined the WAVES on September 7, so I was in Georgia for further training in Storekeepers' School at the time, and oh, how I missed him and my former life.

As always, I found peace by putting my thoughts in rhyme, and although I had forgotten all about the poem, it all came back as I reread it.

Earl's Songs To Me

Lou S. Davidson

There were times when Earl would take his guitar, sit opposite me, and sing love songs to me. How much more could one ask? One time, he wrote new words to the tune of "Beautiful Dreamer," which were forever inscribed in my heart. He has been with the Lord now since '44, but I still hear him singing:

Why are your eyes like sunshine on dew?
Why is the sweetness of heaven in you?
Your charm is holy, simply divine,
You are an angel, but God made you mine.

Heaven is near when you're by my side
All that is precious, in thee doth abide,
Smiling so sweetly, joy bubbling through
You are a vision, my love-dream come true!
You are a vision, my love-dream come true!

There was another one he wrote the words and the music. We had looked at a little cottage and were thinking of buying it, but with the war, he didn't want to leave the burden on me. "If anything ever happens to me . . ." he would say. So we turned it down.

I see a vision of a cute little cottage
Just big enough for us two
Nothing expensive, a couple of rooms
With plenty of fixin' to do.

Perhaps a wee fireplace
At the end of one room
Some green grass, a big tree in view.
I see a vision of a cute little cottage
"Our honeymoon dream home" come true!

Lulu (Merritt) Smythe Davidson
Navy WAVES
1944-1946

Love and Loneliness

Being a Widow

I Miss the Missus

I went out to get the mail one day and was so happy to see one small letter tucked in with all the legal-sized envelopes. However, as I read the printed word *ADDRESSEE*, I realized "That's *me!*" It simply replaced my name! There was no *Mrs.* or anything that would except me from being a child or even a thing. I was so disappointed and felt so unimportant.

I know that many people wonder how one should address a widow. I had read long ago that it is correct to address her as *Mrs.* before her name or even *Mrs.* before her former husband's name unless she has remarried. At the time, I thought, *That's nice to know,* but I didn't realize how it would help to ease the hurt for me later on.

I Miss the Missus

By Lou S. Davidson   ©1994

"Till death do us part, I do"
Had a different meaning then
Hand in hand we'll see it through
And never turn back again.

But now released from that vow
Though we kept it till the end,
And the honored title of *wife*
Is now replaced with *friend*.

First it was *Ms.*, then *Mrs.*
The joy that came with it too
Is gone, along with the title.
I'm addressed now simply as Lou.

A pile of old papers revealed this poem I had written on a small note pad sheet to Earl even though he was "asleep atop the hill." It was composed during the first year I served in the women's service branch, the WAVES.

The "hill" was the Oak Hill Cemetery outside Lemoyne, Pennsylvania. Earl was buried on the crest overlooking the river between Lemoyne and Harrisburg where we spent so much time in *Scotty*, the kayak he had made. When he added a very large sail, he had to make pontoons for it. What fun we had in the evenings to sail out to the little island up the river and enjoy our love. Even though we were married about six years, each encounter was like a new date, whether it was to meet at lunch and then go to the nearby telephone booth to kiss good-bye or in our cozy little apartment where he played his guitar and sang love songs to me as though he were still wooing me.

I always thought of him asleep there on the hill. Each time I tried to tell myself that he was not there—he was in heaven—I would get so upset that I would vow again that someday I would know for sure.

That day came three years later when I asked Jesus to come into my heart. Then I *knew*. Earl had often told me that he thought I had my religion in my head, but I needed Christ in my heart. How right he was! So now I *know* that Earl is in heaven and that someday we will meet again.

Earl had always said that if anything ever happened to him he wanted me to be remarried within three years. After changing our wedding date three times, Ken and I realized that all attempts were futile. (I didn't want to remarry on the anniversary date of Earl's death.) So it was just three years to the day!

Now as I sit alone, I think of the six wonderful years I had with Earl and the forty-three wonderful years I had with Kenny. It's really hard to complain, but I pray that it won't be long before I join them. But perhaps the Lord still has something else for me to do*!*

It's Spring Again

Lou Smythe Davidson   © 1945

Dear Earl:

    It's April and it's spring again!
        Once more the world's in newborn glory.
    The air is crisp yet cooly warm
        But there's a change in this year's story.

    It's time you should begin to plan
        The riggin's for our little craft
    To wash the sail and brightly paint
        The *Scotty* blue from fore to aft!

    It's time that I plant garden paths
        With sweet peas bright and cosmos tall
    Renew the faded cottage sets,
        Put paper on the upstairs hall.

    Its time to pack away our skates
        The last few spins—now memories
    And soon the car top should reveal
        The moonlight shining through the trees.

    So many years, these things, we knew
        This year, the spring has lost its thrill:
    To me in garb of navy blue,
        To you, asleep atop the hill.

EARL'S KAYAK: 1939

If God Had Given Me A Choice

Lou S. Davidson ©1993

If God had given me a choice
    Of which I'd rather had
A short time with a good man
    Or a long time with a bad;

I would not even ask, "How long?"
    For at once I would know
But life with a *wonderful* man
    Is *so awful* when they go!

June the Seventh

Lou S. Davidson   © 1995

Just fifty-six years ago today
    I married Earl, and we stole away
To a cabin on the Jersey shore
    To be together forever more.

But as our love for each other grew
    There were changes in the world anew
And the flaming plane took him away
    With my broken heart, I had to stay.

Then just three years to the very day
    When I could no longer find my way
God sent me Kenny to be my own
    And find the joy I once had known.

For forty-three years, we loved and prayed
    Oh, how I wish he could have stayed,
Now three years later, I sit alone
    And think of the joys that I have *known*.

Diamonds and Opals

Lou S. Davidson   ©1994

You can't compare diamonds and opals
Though both be the number-one grade
Nor put a value on sentiment
Nor can it be scaled by the trade.

The old opal ring of my mother
And the diamond you gave to me
Each has a value beyond its own
That no other person can see.

The first husband God had given me
Then so quickly took him away
In no way clouded my love for you
Nor the joy you brought me each day.

And now, though God has taken you home
I know I've been *marvelously blessed*
I think as I sit here all alone:
HE did give me *two of the best*!

    Since I had enjoyed my own little shop Luart Gifts and Jewels and enjoyed shopping wholesale for friends, I really learned a lot about values.

    Ken was an ex-marine college student when we met, so he was never really happy with the ring he gave me and was glad to be able to get my new one at a price he could afford.

    Then came the time in our lives that other things were so much more precious than diamonds and gems.

Our love for each other,
    Serving the Lord full time,
        Our daughters and sons-in-law
And our gradchildren.
    Now I enjoy our
        great-grandchildren!

Evening

Lou S. Davidson   © 1992

I walk down the beach all alone
      When the sun sinks down past the treetop
And the breakers roar as they come ashore
      They never tire; they never stop.
Oh, they churn and bubble around my feet
      Then return in a quiet roll,
And they seem to say—as they go away,
      "Our God is still in control."

I sing, for I feel you are near
      My cares seem to rise like a vapor
Then you hold my hand as I kick the sand
      Just like a childish caper!
Oh, you seem so near, and you seem so dear
      As in happier days we have known
Then like the wave that I cannot save,
      You are gone . . . and I am alone!

I know I'm not truly alone
      The Spirit of God is within me
And He knows my heart;
      When the teardrops start
He comforts me so patiently:
      He reminds me of my Savior's love
And the love that we will share
      When soon someday, I'll fly away
Together, forever, up there!

I love to sing! I try to keep my mind on the goodness of my heavenly Father, my Lord and Savior. It helps to cope with that awful feeling of loving wife changed to widow's life.

As I sing the old hymns, each one reminds me of a certain time, place, or person. "Jesus Loves Me" always reminds me of Ken. He loved to hear the little ones sing it and often said that it was his favorite. The choir sang it at his funeral along with "In the Garden," his other favorite. I still see his face light up when he was leading the singing in church and someone requested that hymn.

One day, I was singing it, thinking of him, when the tears came down as a flood. They took away the words, but the tune kept right on permeating my mind. It was about evening, and I thought I should get out and go for my walk down the beach. Soon I was singing new words to the old tune, and "Evening" was born.

I wrote the first two verses on the June 11, but each time they came to my mind, I felt rebuked because of the last line. I praise the Lord that *I am not alone*, so I knew that I would have to do something about ending the poem that way.

On June 25, I took a piece of scrap paper and composed another verse. The scrap I used was of last year's appointment book cut into pieces. After some notes and changes, I came up with the third verse. Then I felt better for that is what keeps me going. I'm *not alone* and he's waiting for me in heaven.

The scrap that I used must have been part of the sheet for May 11, 1991. On the bottom of the sheet, I had previously written:

"Kenny went home! Waiting for me."

A Widow's Changed Life

By Lou S. Davidson,   © 1994

When your beloved goes to heaven
>The Word' seems so divine

The blessed hope becomes more blessed
>And His promises more mine.

Without your lover to cling to now
>You reach your hands up to *Him*

And instead of fearing the future
>You find that it's not so dim.

The worldly pleasures cease to please,
>Material things lose worth,

You see all *He* wants you to do,
>And why you're still here on earth!

>*So get busy!*

    As I tried to think of my schedule for the day, I thought of all of the things I would *like* to do and all of the things I *should* do and finally listed all of the things I *must* do. After reading the cards and letters from my friends and loved ones, who serve full-time for my Lord, and as I prayed for each need then read the Word, I was struck with the feeling of being so close to the Lord. I realized how much I could do from praying to witnessing to going, to inviting, etc., and realized that God has been good to me. Although I cannot overcome my grief, nor go back to the way it was, He is taking care of me and has a job for me to do before I can be set free, and in doing so, I find peace.

Reading Psalm 61

Lou S. Davidson   © 1994

"When my heart is overwhelmed"*
I had read again and again.
But life was good, love was full
And joy flowed down like gentle rain.

Now I read that psalm again,
Praying some comfort I might find,
That verse seems to jump out like
A jack-in-the-box in my mind!

For my heart *is* overwhelmed!
But still with gratitude it sings.
I cling to the "higher rock" and
Trusting the covert of Thy wings.

    My heart was overwhelmed by all the pressures I was facing in trying to make the transition of being without Kenny. I was having to adjust to doing all those daily little things alone, in addition to preparing to sell our home and downsize to another location. My Bible reading this morning was Psalm 61. So often, God uses the little *Our Daily Bread** devotional booklet to steer me to just the right message for that day. I found comfort and encouragement from the thoughts written there and in His Word.

---

*   *Our Daily Bread* devotional booklets are published by RBC Ministries. Grand Rapids, MI 49555

My Guest

Lou S. Davidson © 1992

Oh, how I hate to eat alone!
It brings me to despair.
I'll have my Lord to dine with me!
Then I set for Him a chair.

"I know your thoughts," I felt Him say,
"But no need to despair—
For I will always dine with you,
But no need for a chair!"

I mind my manners every meal.
Such peace I've never known!
And since that day, I'm glad to say
I never eat alone!

Beloved Husband and Father
Kenneth Davidson
November 5, 1923
to May 11, 1991

Love and Loneliness

Poems of Ken

Someone New

Lou S. Davidson   ©

So long I had been dead inside
My heart had stopped when my lover died
Though I still lived on.

So long I dreamed of him at night
And constantly from morning light
I realized he was gone.

So many lonely hours I knew
And dreams that never could come true
And then you came.

A great new world you've given me
And my silly heart just leaps with glee
Whenever you speak my name!

My Angel

Lou S. Davidson   © 1947

The trees—how they fly past the windows!
The road slides fast 'neath the car,
The miles, ticking off in succession
All tell me I'm carried afar!
The terrain is now unfamiliar
The weather has turned quite chill
But your parting smile, the look in your eyes
And the thrill of your kiss linger still~
I pray soon to reclaim your caresses
For now I am sure that it's true
Not miles, nor time, nor anyone
Could change my love for you~

Always,

Lou

Ken gave me my engagement ring on Febuary 22, 1947. It was Washington's Birthday. Then it seemed just a day or so till I left to take a previously planned trip to Detroit, Michigan. I had told my friend Helen that I would drive her and her mother to Detroit because she had never driven in the snow, and I had driven many years in the North. I met her when I went to Miami and began working in the same bank. She was going back to her home to be married up there. In fact, she and I had planned to have a double wedding, but we just couldn't work things out.

I recently retraced the trip from the addresses on the letters I sent to Ken while I was away. I had been a widow for nearly three years, and the yearning I had for him I conquered by thinking how wonderful it would be when I returned. It was. He couldn't wait for me to come to Miami, so he drove up to Hollywood to meet me there. I'll never forget that moment in his arms!

Now as I try all methods of curing my anxiety and yearning, I think of that and try to make myself anticipate our meeting again. This time it will not be in Hollywood, Florida, but in heaven.

March 2, 1947

Written in the car between Ocala and Lake City, Florida, on my trip to Detroit.

Ken's Valentine

Lou S. Davidson   © 1946

Darling:

I went to buy a valentine for you, my dear, today
But none of them would say the things I wanted them to say:
They didn't say how grand it is to know how much you care—
The thrill I feel when you hold me close or when you kiss my hair.

They didn't state my love for you or how it lights my day . . .
Your tenderness and fond caress that drives all fear away.
Not one made mention of your eyes or the way they speak to me
By sparkling deep blue depths that only I can see;

How your teasing smile—always there—suspends me, floating in midair
So many things I want to say that none could say or know
That even I can't say myself—so deep inside they go.
So let this be your valentine . . . My dear—I love you *so*!

Lou

While going through some old papers, I found a valentine that I had written to Ken even before we were married. It was dated Febuary 14, 1946; we were married June 7, 1947. There were many more such poems over the years, which have gone by the wayside. However, this one survived.

Happy Birthday, Ken

Lou S. Davidson   © 1946

Happy birthday, darling
    And I'm glad that I'm the one
Who gets your morning kisses
    And your love when day is done.
        I'm glad that I'm the one you chose
           To love you all your life
        To pray with you; be gay with you
           (I'm so proud to be your wife.)
I'm glad that we can always share
    The sun and rain together
To know that we are not alone
    In life's fast changing weather.
        Each tender word you spoke to me
           Is carved upon my heart
        To keep me happy all day long
           When we must be apart.
Your kiss and soft caresses
    Are more thrilling every day
And I love you for your tenderness
    And the little things you say.
        The many, many things you do
           That are just for me alone
        Fill my heart with happiness
           That it has never known
So I wish you happy birthday
    And I thank your mom and dad
And I hope it is the *happiest* one
    That you have ever had!
        All our love, Lou and Spunkin (the dog)

Iron A Shirt

Lou S. Davidson ©1956

When I iron the cuffs and sleeves,
The hardest part,
I think how hard for you
To love me as you do
When all of my faults show through!

When I do the collar stiff,
The important part,
And I feel a deep pride
That love cannot hide
How handsome you'll look by my side.

I fold the shoulder piece,
Be careful on this part,
Straight and strong must be
Yet the strength I see
Is the tenderness you show to me.

The broad back I do next,
There's a lot to this part,
This reminds me of
Your so abundant love
I have time to send a prayer above.

The six-button front,
The tedious part,
One for each day away
But you call just to say
That you love me and brighten my day.

Laundry procedures weren't always as simple as with today's wash-and-wear wardrobes. At the time this poem was written, clothes were dried outside on the clothesline after washing. My iron had no steam setting on it, so cotton dress shirts were prepared for ironing by sprinkling with water and rolling them up. If they couldn't be pressed right away, I stored them in the refrigerator. Hot Florida Sundays required a clean, pressed shirt for my husband both morning and night church services. With three girls and perma-press not yet available, I did a lot of ironing!

Homemade Valentine

Lou S. Davidson   © 1954

To my hubby—

       Here I sit without the car
       Don't even have a dime.
       So how am I 'sposed to buy for you
       A "purty" valentine?!

And so I wrote within a heart:

       Of all the phrases one could write
       From now 'til end of time
       Of all the things that could be done
       Of all the songs to chime
       Not one could ere portray my love
       Nor shout your praises true
       For every day that passes by
       I'm more in love with you.

My First Rose

It Just Takes Time

Lou S. Davidson   ©1995

Daddy showed her the little seeds
As he dropped them into the row
"We'll cover them, and water them—
And soon God will make them grow;
    It just takes time!"

Each day, she went to see the flowers
With disappointment turned away—
Remembering her daddy's words,
He could hear her softly say,
    "It just takes time!"

Then one glad morning, Daddy called
"Come out and see the flower bed."
When she saw the buds and flowers
She looked at him and said,
    "It just takes time!"

Now each new day, I wait and pray
So sad that we must be apart—
My Father tells me He is near
To them with a broken heart.*
    "It just takes time!"

---

*   "The Lord is high unto them that are of a broken heart." (Ps 34:18)

My Husband's Valentine

Lou S. Davidson ©*1951*

A valentine for my husband
Who is still my sweetheart, too,
And the "bestest" daddy in the world,
A bought one just won't do!

You never gripe about my faults
Or stay out late at night.
You kiss away my tears and then
Make everything seem right.

You eat and rave about the food,
Although at times it's pretty bad,
And the way you help with Joy
Makes me very, very glad!

You are a great big he-man,
Yet so sweet and gentle too!
And though we're just old married folks
I'm still in love with you!

Looking Back

Lou S. Davidson   ©1998

As the pastor preached that day
My new husband by my side.
My newborn soul so alive
The sermon topic "Abide."

"Without me, ye can do nothing;
Abide in me, and I in you,"
The pity of those who do not,
And the blessings of those who do.

Then the challenge of the seventh verse*
And the promise for "if we do—"
Would be a verse we would live by
So we vowed to start anew.

We vowed to be true to each other;
We confessed any sins that were there
To live our lives doing His will
Each part of our lives He would share.

Every day began and ended
With Bible reading and prayer
We made our home a home for Him
And all of His people to share.

We attended church, took part in the work
As we did our blessings grew much
We had everything we could use for Him
But no movies, no TV, or such!

We sheltered our children in every way
To be sure their teaching was sound
And for every sacrifice we made
We saw their beauty abound.

Our services in our church and choir
And the Bible lessons we taught
Brought more joy of love and life
Than money could ever have bought.

Our "vines" grew heavy with fruit
As they drew their strength from the vine
I praise the Lord for that vow that day
For no life was more blessed than mine.

Verse John 15:7

---

* "If ye abide in Me, and my words abide in you, ye may ask what ye will and it shall be done unto you" (Jn 15:7).

To Ken

Lou S. Davidson   ©1953

Two little girls so cute and sweet
A cozy home and food to eat

A nice new car and friends galore
A good business partner in your store

Two moms and dads and a grandpa too
Who think there's no one else like you

A wife who loves you more each day
And misses you when you're away

Now with your new specks, you can see
What you couldn't see before
So how could anyone ask for more?

Ode to My Hubby's Picture

Lou S. Davidson   ©1991

The beautiful home you gave me
We shared such a little while;
I still enjoy its beauty,
But, oh, how I miss your smile!

The little ones so dear to us
The children we love so much
Still bring me joy and happiness
But, oh, how I miss your touch!

I know it won't be very long
Till I join you up above;
I try to make you proud of me
But, oh, how I miss your love!

The years have gone*—I'm so alone
Yet the Lord has met my care.
But, oh, how I miss those sacred times
We spent together in prayer!

On the way to the bedroom, as I passed the table with Kenny's picture, I stopped and said, "Good night." Then, as though I were alone in a jungle, I turned on the night-lights, checked the doors, and went to bed. I mumbled something like, "Here I am all alone, left with nothing but a picture."

I knelt at the bedside to pray and ask for safety through the night for me and my loved ones. I was tired from a long day, so I must have found sleep easily.

In the wee hours, I heard a voice speaking very sternly to me. "You are very *ungrateful*! You have so much! You have your beautiful home with no worries about your next meal. You have your children and grandchildren who all love you dearly. How can you say such a thing?"

I raised up, put my feet on the floor, and took pen and paper from the nightstand. By the light of the clock, I penned the first three verses of the poem.

---

*   More than three years later, on August 19, 1994, I was trying so hard to discern the Lord's will and wisdom after many changes in my life since Kenny's passing. I thought of the poem and just felt that I must add another verse.

Ode to My hubby, Ken

Lou S. Davidson   ©1956

I sought a lover brave and true
    Handsome and kind, (as all girls do)
Whose every thought would be of me
    Whose wife I would so proudly be.

But being selfish and unkind
    The perfect mate, I failed to find
Then God in love, reached down to me
    And I met Christ at Calvary.

I saw my true reflection there
    Confessed my sins and in my prayer,
I offered Him the life He bought
    And for His perfect will I sought.

Now as we daily kneel in prayer
    And praise Him for the joys we share
Blessings abundant from above
    Our home and children, perfect love!

I thank Him that the one for me
    (Whose wife I am so proud to be)
Is one who walks by God's own word
    Whose every thought reflects His Lord!

A New Beginning

Lou S. Davidson ©1993

I sat alone and yearned for the day
When God would come and take me away
And once again, I would be with you
Doing the things that we used to do.

But then engrossed in His Holy Word
I read the thing I had often heard
That when we do meet again up there
Where everything's right, and all is fair—

We'll be as angels, from love set free
But you'll be you, and I'll be me
And each will serve the Lord of love
Who paid for our sins and home above.

So from this day on, my dream will be:
Just to take others up there with me.

The Tree Outside My Window

Lou S. Davidson   © 1994

I watched that tree from day to day
      The leaves turned brown and flew away
And as the days went on and on
      I made a vow: "When they are gone,
I'll put away my grief for you
      Forget the past, and start anew."
Each day, the ground bore many more
      My thoughts still of the days of yore
Till just one lingered on the tree.
      Could it know what it meant to me?

The winter past, new leaves arrive
      All happy just to be alive
I'm grateful for their cooling shade.
      What of the vow I once had made?
Still yearning for your love for me
      With broken heart, I watch that tree.
As last year's leaves turned brown and dried
      Reluctantly they all had died—
There's nothing that could make them stay
      God' perfect will made trees that way!

No time, nor leaves, nor old or new
      Can take away my love for you.
I'll *keep* those memories so dear,
      To help me through another year!

To Ken in Heaven

Lou S. Davidson   © 1994

You never wrote a poem to me
As my first boyfriend did.
You never wrote me a love song
As my first hubby did.

But your talent wasn't lacking
Nor was it being hid,
You used it to glorify God
Whenever you were bid.

The congregational singing
So lively with your lead,
When you sang duets or solos
Brought sacred thoughts indeed.

And though you never sang to me,
You met my every need.
When trouble became a burden,
Your prayers would intercede.

You loved your God so fervently,
Then next your family.
And as He blessed your faithfulness,
The blessings fell on me.

So I do not fear tomorrow
Nor what I cannot see.
Just as joy comes out of sorrow
Your love will always be.

(Written in the lobby of the Park Court Hotel, Lancaster Gate, London, July 29, 1994)

The Other Hand

Lou S. Davidson   © 06/13/61

At a June-day wedding, he held my hand
Through times of shadow, held my hand
    Subway stops, mountain rocks
In city crowds or grazing flocks.
    Tilting sailboat, a circus stand
So secure! He held my hand.
    Then just a moment, while apart
Death claimed him, and my broken heart
    Revealed him in an unknown land
A piece of paper in my hand!

Alone! Alone! *So* all alone!
    Where were the stars, the moon that shone?
Searching, searching, searching
    The ever constant search!
People, places, trains, and planes,
    And then somehow, a little church!
The memory of a wedding day
    A hand that held mine all the way
A heart once proud, now at a loss
    Broken, undone, before the *cross*!

A prayer—oh, Lord, help me to pray
    Then it seemed I heard *him* say,
"You would not come before you see,
    There was never any time for *me*."
I raised my hands in ecstasy
    With two strong arms He lifted me
And then I recognized the touch
    I'd never thought of it as such!
His hand in mine, He led the way
    Willingly I followed day by day;

    Now children three and husband to say
    Let's join our hands as we kneel to pray!

Just One More Kiss

Lou S. Davidson   © 1995

He kissed me in the morning
      When he said, "I love you, dear."
He kissed me when he left me
      Or whenever we passed near.

So tenderly he kissed me
      As part of his inmost soul
To blot my tears, calm my fears,
      Or to help me gain control.

He kissed me as he lay there
      When I put my lips to his
I thought back to that first kiss
      Oh! How can it end like this?

How I long for one more kiss!
      As three years turn to four.
All else that I need, I have
      But his kisses are no more!

A Note to Ken

Lou S. Davidson ©1993

Darling Ken,
I went by the hospital again today
But this time it was for me—
The yellow hibiscus was blooming again
And remember that orchid tree?

Well, it was just bursting with beauty and bloom
Flowers of orchid and pink,
It looked much more beautiful than before—
It was happier too, I think.

How can I say I'm happy here without you
Then when we were there before—
Because now you're with Jesus up in heaven
And not suffering at death's cold door.

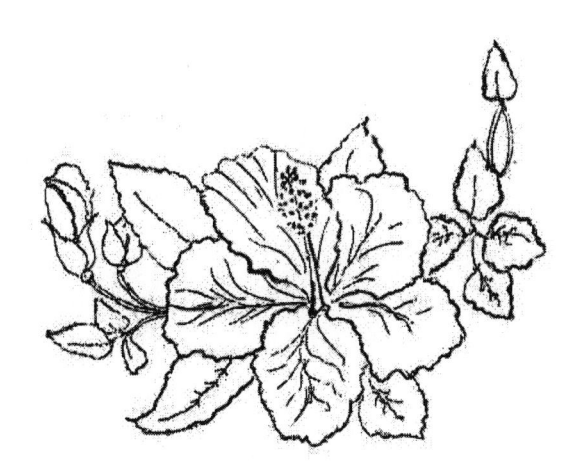

Kenny's Blessing

Lou S. Davidson   © 1994

I never though much of the words he said;
    I just know it brought joy to my heart
As he thanked the Lord for each meal we ate
    Forty-three years, same as the start!

But now that he's gone, and I pray alone
    Grateful to God for His loving care
And I wonder if some of the joy I lack
    Is for the blessing of Kenny's prayer.

He always thanked God for the food He gave
    But were we free from sorrow and strife
Because he always added this phrase:
    "And feed our souls with the Bread of Life."

In Church

Lou S. Davidson   ©2000

We sat together in the pew
The world outside a foreign land
One arm you laid across my back
While the other one held my hand.

The choir robed in angels' garb,
The pastor describing the scene
We were so close ~ so close to God
No care could ever intervene.

But now I sit alone each time
While you're looking down from above
And God Himself sits next to me,
To let me feel your love.

Love of Family
Our Three Girls and Grandchildren

Adopted Love

Lou S. Davidson © 1956

Happy birthday, darling!
How strange it seems to me
That though you are my daughter
Your birth's a mystery.

It doesn't matter, darling
That I wasn't there *that* day
For you're as much a part of me
As the very words I say.

All that really matters is
That God gave you to me
And that I might be the mother
That He would have me be!

A *Mother's Love*

Lou S. Davidson ©1997

Love for a child is a built-in thing
For every mother and dad.
Until trouble comes to a marriage
And all of the good turns bad!

My father left my mother alone
And she went to work each day.
I was cared for by another.
That lady needed her pay.

Mother became ill and could not work
So she cried out to the Lord.
"My baby needs more love and care
Than I can ever afford."

He heard her prayer and the answer came,
"There is nothing else to do;
I know someone who will take the child
Who will truly love her too."

Now many years have come and gone
There is this that I can say,
"I know how much she loved me . . .
Enough to give me away."

Thinking about Joy's adoption, this poem was written as though *she* would have written it. I was reflecting on how much love it took for a mother to give her baby for adoption. Surely, the mother was blessed to see how her sacrifice provided that baby she loved so much a wonderful life with other loving parents.

Joy's Sunday School Shoes

Lou S. Davidson   ©1952

She's still asleep ~ the sleepyhead!
And there beside her on the bed
Those old worn-out
Sunday school shoes.

Last Christmas, they were shining new
Patent leather and buckles too!
Her first pair of
Sunday school shoes.

She now can buckle them herself
And though new white ones line the shelf
They are still her
Sunday school shoes.

Donadeane's Healing

Lou S. Davidson c 1995

"A year or more," the doctor said.
    But we were glad she could be healed.
"The bone will grow to proper size
    For the space the x-rays revealed."

As I cradled her in my lap
    All rolled up in those straps so tight
They seemed to squeeze my heart as well.
    "Oh, Lord," I said, "could this be right?"

I begged Him for a month or two
    Or for some time less than a year!
Then He said, "Just ask me for *now*!"
    My heart was filled with godly fear!

"Yes, heal her *now*, oh, God, I pray,
    Oh please, God hear my earnest plea
And heal this child, Lord, she's your child
    For we have given her to thee."

I could hardly wait to tell Ken
    And he knew just what we should do
He called the pastor—we all prayed
    With oil, he anointed her too.

We could not know of God's answer
    By faith, Ken said, "Take that thing off!"
We praised the Lord for His goodness
    But there were others who would scoff!

So we went again to the doctor
    Where her condition first was known
He took new x-rays, then he said,
    "The bone is *completely grown*"!

When reading my Bible one March morning in 1995, I read about Moses praying for Miriam's *immediate* healing in Numbers 12:13. Those words he prayed resounded in my head and heart. I thought back to March 1952 when I too had said those very words: "Heal her now, oh, God." Just as God answered Moses with a miracle, He did the same for me. I have never forgotten the awe of hearing God speak to me.

I praise the Lord for not only making her leg bone grow but also for actually sparing her life! She was miraculously delivered because the doctor had removed *three* loops of the umbilical cord from her neck. This was preventing her from getting nourishment and perhaps why the hipbone had not fully grown. She was two months early and weighed only four pounds, four ounces, then dropped to three pounds, twelve ounces. She remained in the hospital in an incubator for several months. God had a plan, however, for her to be a special part of our family. She is a real walking miracle and has been a blessing to her family and many others throughout her lifetime!

'Neath the Shadow of the Cross

Lou S. Davidson   ©1971

*A wedding song written especially for Donadeane,
our second daughter, and her husband, Don Paulison
May 29, 1971*

'Neath the shadow of the cross
I pledge my love to you
Henceforth from now forever,
Undying, ever true.
'Neath the shadow of the cross
Where God's beloved Son
Was crucified for our sins
We both become as one.

Born again by faith in Him
From Satan's pow'r set free
You are the answer to my prayer.
He made you just for me.
'Neath the shadow of the cross
We pledge to Him alone
Our lives to take the Gospel
To those who've never known.

And when He calls us home
May we not suffer loss,
But present the crowns we've gathered
In the shadow of the cross.

It is now 2008, and they are still happily married and serve the Lord faithfully in their church. They gave me a grandson, Daniel, who has now married and given me a great-granddaughter, Samantha.

Continue in My Word

Lou S. Davidson   © 1963

*This morning as I drank His Word
And His Spirit warmed my soul,
He drove me to my knees in prayer
Till the tears began roll.*

*Oh, how I begged to know His will
For wisdom and strength to do
The task that He has given me
And for grace to see it through.*

*Oh, how I longed to be near him
And to hold His pierced hand.
So desperately, I need Him!
How I longed for a clear command!*

*Then by faith, I felt His presence
And heard His voice so sweet,
"Just follow me and trust in me,
My Word will guide your feet."*

*With a long, deep sigh, I arose.
Then with my eyes still blurred
I found everything I needed
As I continued in His Word.*

Ken and I wanted our children to learn to read well early and have Christian teachers. The one large Christian school in the city at that time purchased land in the opposite direction of where we lived. A group of other Christians, believing as we did in the need for another school at our end of town, worked toward making it a reality. At the last minute, the project was abandoned.

Feeling the need so strongly, I was led to take the position of directing a New Christian school in the northern part of the city. I depended daily on the Lord for His help and His wisdom. James 1:5 says, "If any of you lack wisdom, let him ask of God." I wore out that verse! Never receiving a paycheck from the school, Ken and I made up the slack for the school's expenses from his salary many times. Previously, I was a bookkeeper but never had to supply the funds, drive children, clean the building, file government reports, and hire teachers, among many other things! Our teachers made a real sacrifice financially to teach at the school.

The years of directing the school gave me a day-by-day reliance on the wisdom of God. Without His leading and guiding, the North Miami Christian School would never have been

For Ginni

Lou S. Davidson   ©1970

She called us mommy and daddy, but little could she know
How great the love we held for her or all that made it so.
So many things our hearts desired to lavishly expend
Yet we know that love and holiness paid a greater dividend.

Through fever, colic, and braces, through tears and sorrow too,
The love and tenderness we shared, with joy, we saw it through.
The times we corrected or punished or challenged and taught and prayed,
She could not know we were building the life she has now displayed.

Though we longed to hold her closely and keep her by our side,
We knew through limitless boundaries our love would still abide.
She gave us all we could dream of, the joy could never be told!
Her love is more precious than rubies, her smile—than silver or gold.

We gave her a love for her Savior and taught her His words and ways.
And know that she'll always be kept by His hand through all her days.
But our greatest gift to our baby as we tenderly turn her loose,
Is the life so pure and heart so true to present Him for His use.

This poem was written in 1970 to our youngest daughter when she attended Toccoa Falls Academy in Georgia, where she gained new independence and experiences that changed her life.

The Story of Paul's Hibiscus
Lou S. Davidson   © 1990

We were visiting Paul and Ginni
The winter of eighty-nine,
I looked at his beautiful flowers
And one just had to be mine!

> A sketch of this lovely hibiscus
> Before the children arrive
> Then I'll have a living example
> When it's no longer alive.

Then someday, I'll paint it for P. J.
To frame and hang on his wall,
Then I left it there on the table
Through supper, devotions, and all . . .

> When I saw it there the next morning,
> The bud that had once unfurled
> And blossomed full in its beauty
> Had also, in beauty, recurled.

What beauty for such a short life
Could only God, the Creator, afford;
Who could guess that just a year later,
> Our Paul would be with the Lord!

(In loving memory of Rev. Paul James DeStefanis, 1953-1990)

See front cover for painting of the Paul's open hibiscus

New Verse to an Old Hymn

Lou S. Davidson   © 1987

Amazing grace, amazing love
Now fills my ransomed soul.
I once was torn by sin and scorn
But now I am made whole.

And when my earthly tour is done
And I shall see His face ~
I pray He'll say, "Well done, my son,"
Oh, what *amazing grace*!

This was written for Rev. Paul J. DeStefanis, first husband of our youngest daughter, Ginni. God blessed Paul with a wonderful voice. They traveled for Miami Christian University for three years. Paul preached and sang to many congregations throughout his short lifetime here on earth.

Dearest Ginni

Lou S. Davidson   ©1978

Some of our blessings
    Are greater than another
But one of the greatest
    Is to be a mother.

So now you have Vinny
    What more can I say
Than have a *happy*
    first Mothers' Day

        Love, Mom

(Written under the hair dryer at your other mother's beauty shop)

Reunion at the Horizon

Lou S. Davidson ©1990

Heaven seems far up over your head
The earth under your feet—so near
You wonder why he has gone ahead
And left you alone down here.

Look down the road—how it seems to rise
And the sky rolls down like a shade;
So never lose that love in your eyes
The faith in your heart will not fade!

Start every day with a fervent prayer
And He'll let your journey be sweet.
Soon you will reach the end of the road
Where heaven and earth always *meet*.

(Written for Ginni, with sympathy, after Paul's death in 1990.)

Thank You

To all of you who surrounded us
With your prayers or gifts of love
During those days of aching hearts
When our Paul was called above,
We give our heartfelt, fervent thanks
Insufficient though it seems
But we ask the Lord to *bless you*
Beyond your wildest dreams.

"The *blessing of the Lord*
it maketh rich, and He addeth NO sorrow with it."—Proverbs 10:22

(This was written on thank-you cards to friends after Paul's death.)

Happy Birthday, Daughter

By Lou S. Davidson   © 2001

In all the world,
Like you is no other,
And I'm so glad
That I'm your mother!

The love of God
That shows on your face
Just makes the world
A much better place.

Love and prayers,
Mom

Our three daughters' birthdays are all in a row, two weeks apart, beginning with Donadeane's on January 27, then Joy's on February 18, and Ginni's on February 27! We start off each year with lots of cake and celebrating!

This year, this poem was in their cards I made.

The Marriage Braid
by Lou S. Davidson   ©1990

Take two cords and twist them tight
Hold the top with all your might.
Yet neither of the two will stay
But each will go its separate way.

Then take a third and braid the three
And try again and you will see:
To think it parts them is absurd,
They're held together by the third.

So when you choose God's very best
Take Jesus also—as your guest.
Then as within your lives, He weaves
He'll guide you o'er your troubled seas.

Tracy and Billy
June 17, 1994

I was honored this poem was used for the occasion of my first grandson's wedding. I wanted to convey the truth that any marriage could weather any storm if the couple allowed God to be in charge and guide them.

The poem was engraved on a lovely floral paper complementing the wedding colors and given to guests for a memento. Three narrow ribbons of contrasting colors were attached to the top corner of the card to symbolize the bride, groom, and the Lord. Guests could see the reality of the first two verses firsthand!

The poem was shared with guests again six months later when Melody (my first granddaughter) and Keith Young were married.

Tiffany's Card

Lou S. Davidson   ©1997

I would love to pick up all my love for you
And send it to you
But the UPS truck is too small!

I would love to send you a much bigger check,
But my bank account says,
"That's all!"

I would love to gather my prayers for you
and send them all your way—
But instead I'll keep them here and
Send them to God each day!

Tiffany, Ginni's daughter, lived here in Georgia with us until she moved back to Florida for a job opportunity. I miss her.

Happy February 14 to My Family

Lou S. Davidson ©1992

Roses are red, violets are blue
To buy a valentine for each of you
Then add five stamps therewith to send
Is somewhat more than I can spend.

So cash the check down at the bank
Sometime before next Monday
And get all the fixings to prepare
For each, a hot fudge sundae!

Love for everyone!

Sometimes Daddy Must Say "No"

Lou S. Davidson © 1993

I could not give the child the knife,
> Though I knew she wanted it so;
But someday she will understand
> There are times when Daddy must say 'no'

I know it's hard to count the days
> When you're seven turning eight,
But someday soon he'll understand
> There are times when Daddy must say 'wait'

Sometimes they have a certain need
> Or a desire—and I confess:
Daddy gets the greater joy
> Those times when Daddy can say 'yes.'

So as I pray so fervently
> For my urgent need to be met
It may be yes, or no, or later
> But my God hasn't failed me yet.

And after years of answered prayer
> Although I had not planned it so
'Twas for His Glory and my good
> Those times when Daddy did say no!

Once again, I am in a place where I need the impossible, so as I pray and ask my God to work it all out, I realize that He may just say "No—It's not *my* will just now." I can accept that knowing that if He does say *no*, it will be for my good and His glory. Then I thought, *Perhaps He will say, 'Yes, but not now'* or *It would be so wonderful if He just said yes!*

As I remembered the many, many times over the past (nearly fifty) years, He always answered our prayers. Later, we could look back and see very clearly *why* He answered as He did, and we were so glad that He had the foresight to be able to answer that way.

Then I thought of times when our children or grandchildren wanted something, and Kenny had to deny it. He would come to me for solace of the hurt, knowing that I agreed wholeheartedly with him. Then there were times when he could give them what they asked or even surprise them, and then the joy we shared together was usually so much greater than the joy the child received in obtaining his or her desire.

Love of Family

Family and Friends

God blessed us with wonderful, extended families.
Ken's side included a loving, supporting father-in-law and
mother-in-law who welcomed me into their family from the start.
His grandfather was living at the time of our marriage also.

My family was a large one, compared to Ken's being an only child.
My parents were thrilled at our marriage and visited our home often.
Ken enjoyed my two sisters and three brothers and their respective
families through the years. God gave us many good times together.

Many friends have been like family too! Through sad times and glad
times, lean times and plenty, I'm thankful good Christian friends
have always been there for us.

Dear Mother

Lou S. Davidson

I wish that I could bring to you
This happy Christmas Day
All the things I thought you'd like
While shopping on my way

I wish we could invite you all
To come and dine with us
With linen white and candlelight
And entertain you thus!

I wish I could have made for you
Something your very own,
With loving thoughts in every stitch
As my love for you has grown.

But if we could afford to do
These things I've named above,
And had all the wealth of every land
And did not have your love
We would indeed be sad!

And so we bring our gift of love
And thank the Lord for you
And pray the things we cannot give
He'll give and do for you!
And hope you will be glad!

This was written to my Mother after Dad was with the Lord. Mother was living with my younger sister, Vera, and her husband, Ken, in New Jersey. Now they are all with the Lord.

Happy Birthday, Mother

Lou S. Davidson   ©1952

Nothing we could give to you
Could ever quite express
The way we feel or appreciate
Your love and tenderness.

Nothing we could say to you
In any word or rhyme
Could let you know how much we care
Or our love for you sublime.

So we just wish you happy birthday
Which will top off any other
And thank our God that we have you
For our own precious Mother!

Lou

Mother

Lou S. Davidson

She dreams again this Mothers' Day
Of years that have gone by
Of happy days with you in arms,
No cloud to dim her sky.
She picked you up so many times,
A tired, drooping head
And sang her babe to sleep with hymns,
Then put you in your bed.
She kissed you, loved you, held you close
And dried your falling tears.
She prayed that God would save and keep
And guard you through the years.

Though years have gone since that first day
She looked into your face;
Her heart rejoices now to know
God saved you by His grace.
Thank God, today with all your heart
For mothers' love and care
In helping you to know the Lord,
And teaching you in prayer.
How fortunate that girl or boy
Whose parents love the Lord
And strive to walk each day with Him
In loving full accord.

Little White Church

Lou S. Davidson   ©

In a little white church
I found the Lord,
And gave my life to Him
And all the pleasures of the world
Faded and grew dim.

In a little white church
I found your son
And I gave my heart to him
And now it is full of love
Up to the brim.

In a little white church
When we kneel to pray,
We thank our God for you
And for each other
And the day I found that little white church!

(Written to Mother Davidson.)

Oh, Death, Where is Thy Sting?

Lou S. Davidson   © 1956

The message of death fell hard on my heart!
For comfort, I went to His Word,
To rest in the precious promises there
Perhaps to find one I'd not heard.

The account of the *Rapture*[†] I read again
And the Psalms, I leafed through thoughtfully.
Then He gave me a verse—my soul did sing,
For it proved all sufficient to me!

Precious to him is the death of his saints[‡]
And I thought just *how* precious, through grace
One that *He* loved and redeemed by His blood
Could now praise Him *face-to-face*!

When Mother Davidson went to be with Lord, I was devastated. She was a loving mother-in-law, treating me as the daughter she never had. I learned so much about practical family life as well as drawing from her steady, stalwart Christian testimony. I learned from her of mealtime prayers. She taught me many kitchen tricks as well as reminding me that washing dishes or peeling potatoes was also prayer time. Her Christian love was evident in her care of family and friends. Her church attendance was consistent though she attended without her husband. She grounded her son in Christian principles, which contributed to the beauty of our marriage. I was very brokenhearted at her passing and turned to my newfound faith in God, which she had encouraged and prayed for, to find comfort.

[†]   1 Thesssalonians 4:13-18
[‡]   "Precious in the sight of the Lord is the death of His saints" (Psalm 116:15).

Loving Thoughts on Mothers' Day

Lou S. Davidson

For Mother Merritt:

> *Dear Mother . . .*
>
> *You think that you're the lucky one*
> *This is your day and all the fun*
> *But think how lucky we are too*
> *'Cause we're the kids you're the mother to!*

For Mother Davidson:

> *Dear Mother . . .*
>
> *You know how much I love my mommy,*
> *How much she means to me.*
> *And yet here is a mystery*
> *That never clear will be:*
> *How God could ever give me*
> *Such a perfect lover*
> *Who also had a precious mom*
> *To be my other mother!*

To Mother Merritt in the Hospital

Lou S. Davidson © 1966

We called in this get well greeting to Mother in the hospital in New Jersey.
Each family member wrote a verse, including the pet cat!

From Lou: Instead of sending you flowers today
                    We called to give a poetic bouquet.
                    Here's a hibiscus of radiant hue
                    To tell of our prayers and our love for you!

From Ginni: I will send roses, the talisman,
                    To tell you exactly what's on my mind.
                    I love you, dear Grandma, and hope you will be
                    All better soon to come see me!

From Donadeane: I will send pansies with cute little faces,
                    Smiling at you as your illness erases.
                    Every night we pray for you and ask the Lord
                    To sell your house too!

From Joy: A carnation I send with petticoat edges
                    And nice green leaves from off the hedges.
                    Sorry you're sick, Grandmother dear,
                    Get better quick and come down here!

From Ken: Roses are red, violets are blue,
                    Sugar is sweet and so are you!

From Tiptoe: I will send catnip to tickle your tummy,
                    Because I'm a cat, I think it's yummy!
                    I'll climb down out of my favorite tree,
                    And purr real pretty when you come and see me.

The Anniversary Plaque

Lou S. Davidson   © 1973

To Mommy and Daddy

By your love, you taught me to love
Your tenderness taught me to care,
Your faith in action taught me to trust,
Your unselfishness taught me to share.

From my youth, you taught me to pray
And of the God who answers prayer
Whenever I needed someone
You were always there.

This was written in gold on a porcelain plaque, which I painted with violets and edged in gold for their sixtieth anniversary.

How thankful I am for my parents and their love.

The Lost Poem

Lou S. Davidson   © 1956

When I was just a teenage child
     God called my baby sister home
And the hurt that dwelt within my heart
     Flowed through my pen into a poem.

Now many years have come and passed
     Healed the scar and dried the tears
Alas! En route my changing life
     Those precious lines *lost* with the years!

In vain, I search my memory
     Oh, would I could recall
The lines that told of childhood plans
     (I should have memorized it all!)

But I recapture just the end
The first part I may never know
Those lines that laid my heartache bare
"My heart's with her, beneath the snow."

I was trying to remember the poem that I wrote about my little sister Irene Shirley when I was a teenager. The fact that it has been sixty-eight years since I wrote it, I decided that if I couldn't think of the original, that I would write another about the things I still remembered of that unforgettable day!

Little by little, I came up with what I thought would be acceptable, but I really wasn't happy with it. If only I could find a copy of the original! However, all of my old papers had been stored in my parents' basement while I was in the WAVES, and the flood ruined them all.

While I was contemplating the fact that my poem about her untimely death would have to be lacking in my book, the phone rang.

My sister-in-law, Evelyn, was on the phone. She asked what I was doing, and when I told her, she said, "Oh! I have that poem. Get a pencil and paper while I go get it." In minutes, she was back and read it to me. I wrote it, and as each line came alive in my heart, I wanted to scream, "THANK YOU, LORD." Now I have the lost poem! Let me share it with you. Note change of my name.

Reminisce

By Lulu Marion Evelyn Merritt   © 1935

It's snowing now, it snowed that day
My sister died and went away;
The downy flakes that float aroun'
Blowing upward, falling down
Blocking all—chasing gloom
Just as it fell upon her tomb.

Long years ago, yet recently
As yesterday, it seems to me
Though tears are dried, flowers gone
That fateful day
Will linger on
Makes no matter where I go
My heart's with her
Beneath the snow.

(Irene Shirley Merritt was born October 4, 1934, and died January 5, 1935.)

We had a family in our church in Miami, Florida, who left to move out to the northwest area of the United States. The children had never seen snow before and were really enjoying their first big snowstorm. However, as they dug a hideaway in the snowbank, they had no idea that it would collapse and bury them alive. By the time they were found, it was too late. They were already with the Lord.

When we received the word, we were brokenhearted, and once again, I poured out my feelings in a poem:

A Heaven Without Children

Lou S. Davidson ©

I dreamt I entered heaven's gates
And all was bright and fair
But I was disappointed for
There were no children there!

A heaven without children?
Oh! Surely 'twas not so!
I went to ask my Savior, "Why?"
I knew that He would know.
"There were none I could find," He said,
"To give their child to me
Lest feeling that my love for them
Had somehow ceased to be."

Then I awoke, remembering
Those with grateful hearts in love
Gave back to Him, the gift He gave
Till they meet again above!

A Friend
Is One You Can Ask

By Lou S. Davidson   © 1984

To go to the airport at four in the morning;
To do your wash when your
        machine's on the blink;
To watch over your home
        when you're on vacation;
To help fix the leak down under the sink!

To take in your children
        when you run late shopping,
To come pray with you
        when the going is rough;
To mow your lawn
        when you're not physically able
To lend you the diff'rence
        till you have enough.

But a *special friend*
        just looks at the task
And says, "Let me do it."
        before you can ask!

You are a *special friend to me*!

    Over the years, there have been several who have fit these situations, and I praise the Lord for each one. So often, they were widows or single moms and often the man next door.

    There were times when one of us could do for the other, but when we were both going to the airport to leave on a trip abroad for a month, when we were miles away from our families, when Ken had his health problems, etc., God always sent a *dear friend*!

Proverbs 17:17 says, "A *friend* loveth at all times."

The Surprise Gift

Lou S. Davidson   © 1995

For years, we supported missions
>And missionaries were our friends
We always tried to show our love
>Which develops as friendship wends.

Then we moved to live among them
>As volunteers to serve their needs
How our hearts were warmed so often
>As they helped *us* with loving deeds.

One day, we had our chimney cleaned
>But had no money left for wood
The next day out on our terrace
>What a precious gift there stood!

Since then, the years have come and gone
>And neighbors still are very good
But I'll never forget the sight
>Of that wheelbarrow filled with wood!

When Ken and I were working with Wycliffe at JAARS as volunteers, we had bought a home and were delighted that it had a fireplace.

Before we could use it, however, we were told that we should have the chimney cleaned. That we did and were anxious to enjoy the fire. However, Ken said, "While that took the rest of our money, now we don't have enough to buy wood until the first of the month." I must have mentioned this to our neighbors because the next day when we woke up and looked outside, there on the porch was a wheelbarrow loaded with wood.

This was just another way that we found by giving all to follow Him, that He would provide all our needs.

Love of Family
Fun and Fanciful

A B C Poem

Lou S. Davidson © 1990

A is for ADAM, the first man God made
  In His own image in Eden's cool shade.

B is for the BIRDS so high in the air
  God made the fifth day and keeps in His care.

C is for CHILDREN, God's gift to mankind
  In many sizes and colors you'll find.

D is for DANIEL, who bowed not to men
  And God kept him safe in the lions' den.

E is for EVERYONE, large or just small
  All the world over, and God loves them all.

F is for FRIENDSHIP with someone we like
  To tell a secret or to share our bike.

G is for GIFTS that we all like to get
  To be the GIVER is much better yet.

H is for HOLY, as God's holy name
  His people, His church, we treat just the same.

I is for INFANT, the Son of God came
  To die for our sins and give us His name.

J is for JESUS, God's gift to receive
  The *one* requirement is "truly believe."

K is for KEEPING the door of your doubt
  Which lets *truth* come in and keeps *evil* out.

L   is for the LAW, an order or rule
         That we should obey at home or at school.

M   is for ME and God made me, I know
         His purpose I'll find as I learn and grow.

N   is for NOAH, by God's instruction
         Obeyed and was saved from great destruction.

O   is for OBEY that your days be long and each trial that comes be turned into song.

P   is for PATIENCE, a fruit we all seek
         To be *quick* to hear, and yet *slow* to speak.

Q   is for QUIET for a time each day
         To spend with your Lord to brighten your way.

R   is for RIGHTEOUS or right in God's sight
         But unconfessed sin will keep out the light.

S   is for SATAN, the father of lies.
         The god of all sin in clever disguise.

T   is for TRUSTING in what we believe
         Like faith in action that we may receive.

U   is for UNION, like the three-in-one,
         The Holy Spirit, the Father, and Son.

V   is for VERILY Jesus so often said,
         It means "it is true" those things which we read.

W   is for WOMEN, especially wives
         Whose husbands love them as much as their lives.

X   is for a SIGN that means wrong or here,
         Or even a kiss from one who is dear.

Y   is for YOU—what will your end be?
        Will you be with Christ for eternity?

Z   is for ZERO and that shall be all
        You can take with you at the trumpet's call.

So heed the word *come*; come to Jesus today.
    Come just as you are, He loves you that way.
        He loved you so much, He died for your sin,
            So open your heart, and let Him come in.

This poem was taken from my book *Barbilet, How To Teach The Bible By Teaching Art*.

And God Said

Lou S. Davidson   © 1994

When God created heaven and earth
He said, "Let there be light"
For all was dark and without form
And then the world was bright!

On day two did He divide
The waters that were seen
He put some up and some below
A firmament between.

On day three did He call out
The dry land from the seas
And then to make a pretty scene
He added grass and trees.

Then on day four, four things He called
The sun, moon, stars at night
He used them to establish time
As well as for their light.

Then on day five came fish and fowl.
All creatures of the sea
And all that fly above our heads,
Some grounded, such as we.

Then on day six, God made a pair
Of cattle, beast, and man
And creeping things all made of dust
To finish out His plan.

He admired His great creation,
All He had invested.
It was the perfect universe.
So the seventh day, He rested!

I am fascinated by the *power in God's voice*! He *spoke* and it happened! What a beautiful creation H*e* made from nothing just by *speaking*! Then I think of the new creation He made of me just because of *my* speaking. The fact that Christ suffered and died on the cross to pay for my sin did not change me one bit. I had to open my mouth and confess my sin and my belief and ask Jesus to come into my heart. Then I too became a new creation. 2 Corinthians 5:17

Bus Ride Through the Alps

Lou S. Davidson   ©1993

Through a tunnel, over a bridge—for miles and miles we go
Then through a tunnel and over a bridge—with a river down below!

The mountains all around us rise—but the bus goes straight along
Through a tunnel and over a bridge—and we all join in song.

No whirling road up to the top—then round and round back down;
We tunnel through the crested part—and *over* the little town.

We meet our joys, then our foes—our share of troubles, we know
But as we pray and serve our Lord—hand in hand with him we go.

He tunnels through the height of pain—he spans the sorrow deep
He helps us through each trying day—then gives us peaceful sleep.

Then when our journey's end is nigh—and through the veil we pass
He'll take us up with Him on high where all is smooooth as glass!

    The second time Ken and I went to Europe, we went with the Greater Europe Mission Tour. It was great! As we journeyed by bus all through the Alps, we were impressed with the *flat* road all the way!

    Having taken many a vacation through the mountains of North Carolina and that area, I remembered the *spiral* we took up to the top, then the *spiral* we took on the way down, 'til we reached our destination. Then I noticed that we were going through the peaks and over the valleys! Thus I sat peacefully viewing the scenery, singing hymns, or even reading.

    Now it is 1993 as I sat alone the other night, too tired to do more. I flipped the whizzer and came to the travel program. To my amazement, I recognized the area and watched as the bus went through a tunnel, then over a bridge, then again and again!

    I likened it to the way our Lord takes us on our way: He smoothes out high crests of challenges and the valleys of disappointments by His presence, taking us on our way.

Cherry Blossoms in DC

Lou S. Davidson   © 1993

Cherry blossoms abloom in DC
Hold bittersweet memories for me:
> Their beauty was such
> Almost too much
The aroma fell so full and free;

Their boughs would fall o'er the pathway
I walked at the close of each day
> My hubby was gone
> I was alone
But their beauty took all care away.

There was something strange as I recall
The blossoms fade, and then they fall
> But from each shoot
> Was never *fruit*
They had their beauty, and that was all!

Then I looked to Him, their Creator
I prayed to find something much more
> He has met my need
> Now I sow seed
That it might bear fruit up in *His* store.

    The other day I was flipping the channels to find something fit to watch when I caught just a glimpse of the Capitol building in Washington DC with a large branch of the cherry blossoms in front of it. That was a scene I had enjoyed many times in World War II when I was stationed there as a WAVE. I flipped back quickly, but it was gone. As I gave up on TV amusement again, I thought of the beauty I enjoyed as I walked that pathway around the Reflection Pool with the Washington Monument at one end and the Lincoln Memorial at the other. Depending upon the time of day, and the location of the sun shining upon the monuments, they took turns reflecting their beauty into the pool.

I thought too of the way beauty, especially God-made beauty, can wipe away sorrowful thoughts and bring peace of mind. Oh, if only we could always think on beautiful things! When I look back and reminisce about the fact that I was a widow, twenty-seven years old, with a horrible yearning in my heart, and yet how God drew me to Himself, gave me new life and peace. Later He gave me a new husband and much happiness. For forty-three years we enjoyed each other, our families, our children, grandchildren all living close to the Lord.

Now that I am replaying the role of widow, I think back to the first time. I was like the cherry blossoms in DC—all beauty but no fruit! Now my time is taken by trying to create God's beauty in such a way that others can enjoy it in paintings, teaching art, etc., but mostly by bringing new life to those who do not know Christ personally or helping those who do. The *fruit* of the Spirit, according to Galatians 5:22-23, is "love, joy, peace, longsuffering, gentleness, goodness, faith, meekness and temperance." I find that as I walk in the spirit (Gal. 5:25), He manifests this fruit in and through me.

Green Apples

Lou S. Davidson   ©1952

Did you ever climb an apple tree
With a saltshaker in your hand?
Then walk around on the branches
Till you found one you could stand

Then find a place wide enough to sit
And enjoy your first big bite
And spit it out as fast as you can
And lap a little salt from your hand
To take the tartness down.

Now you salt, then bite, then savor
Till you're down to the core
And you look around at the others
To try to find one more
Of all the other apples
Ripe and delicious fruit
That you'll enjoy at a later time.

You forget, but the ones you
Sweetened by salting
Before their time had come
You'll remember long after
The years have come and gone.

Shadows

Lou S. Davidson © 1990

I love to see the colors changing
Where shadows fall from trees so tall
In the morning light, they stretch so far
At noon, a ring beneath is all.

Where fence posts stagger up the hill
A certain boundary to recall,
Their shadows lying down beside them
Seem to be tempting them to fall.

In the evening, the shadows lengthen
And fall to the opposite side
Then darkness chases, then erases
Them all, for now 'tis eventide.

The Budding Artist

Lou S. Davidson   © *1995*

He wanted to paint the village scene
But try as he would, it looked dark and mean.
So he cast it down and tried again
But the muddied sky made it look like rain!

Then he said, "I think I'll try something new!
I'll go to the ocean and paint the view!"
And his old shrimp boat looked just like that,
But the water just wouldn't lie down flat!

So he cast it with the rest of the pack
And said, "I give up! I don't have the knack!"
But one came by and looked at the mess
And said, "You must be quite close to success!
If fifty failures will pave the way
To learn all you need, this could be the day!"

To make water lie down and the sky go away
You dull the colors as we call "grey,"
Things decrease as they go farther back,
It's not skill you need! Its *knowledge* you lack!

So he said, "I'll give it another try."
He went to the pile. "Oh, that's a good sky—
And in this one, the water looks wet,
I'll use this style and make a vignette.

"This one has that mossy old tree,
And this one shows good depth to the sea.
These shadows seem to fall just right,
And this one has that glimmer of light.

"This old shrimp boat looks pretty true,
For my point of interest, that would do!"
So he gathered each one, and wonders never cease,
Combined them all in a grand masterpiece!

The Maple Tree

Lou S. Davidson   ©1987

The maple tree
Fascinates me!
The craziest thing I've seen.

It comes in in red
And goes out in red

But wears yellow and green
In between!

Having spent many years in Florida,
I'm really enjoying Georgia's changing seasons.

The Solution

Lou S. Davidson   ©2001

For the wrinkle, there's the iron;
        For the awful, there's the good;
        For the distance, there's the auto
        For the fire, there's the wood.

For the tongue, there's no taming
        Says James's theology
But for the gripping and the blaming,
        There is still *apology*.
    PRAISE THE LORD!

John 3:8-10

You're Just A Bird

Lou S. Davidson   ©1993

You have no crested head,
    No song, have I heard,
No red breast like the robin,
    You are just a bird!

But you fly above me;
    For God gave you wings;
You eat berries from the tree
    God's provided things.

When I look at other birds
    I'm so much aware
Of all their vivid colors
    Not who put them there.

So you are just a bird!
    Doing what birds do
But you make me think of God
    While I'm watching you!

And I am just like you
    No great sight to see,
Oh, may people think of God
    When they look at me.

It was a nice, cool morning, so I took my breakfast and went out on the porch. As I watched the birds come and go, a beautiful cardinal came and left; then a beautiful blue jay came, pushed the others away, took a beak-full, and flew away showing his beautiful black-and-white markings on the bright blue. I thought, *He's so pretty, he's snooty!*

Two red-headed woodpeckers who call that tree their own continued flying out to the feeder, grabbing their seeds, and quickly finding shelter inside the branches so that I could not admire their beauty.

All the time there was another bird, down on the ground picking up what the others dropped. Then it flew to the Florida holly tree to enjoy the berries God had put there. I thought, *Isn't it wonderful how God enables them to fly?* Then I noticed my bird came back again and, between pecking, seemed to look into the porch as though he were thanking me for the goodies I had put there. I found out later that it was a dove.

Unlimited Potential

Lou S. Davidson ©1997

Of all the books that have been written
Or will be from now on
Of every word that has been spoken
From ages past and gone;

For every thought that was put to word
In poetry or prose,
Or those that were kept within the mind
So no one ever knows;

God gave us just twenty-six letters
And that was all it took
To speak one's thoughts to someone else
Or write them in a book!

Little Rhymes Included In Cards Over the Years

Lou S. Davidson   © 2008

I can't begin to tell you
What your friendship means to me;
You are such a good example
Of what a Christian's ought to be.
So have a Happy birthday
And thank God every day
Continuing to serve Him
As you go along your way.

I can't begin to tell you
What your friendship means to me.
You are such a good example
Of what a Christian's ought to be.
So keep on keeping on
And praise God every day,
Continuing to serve Him
As you go along your way.

I miss you when you're not in church,
And I'm sure that He does too!
He wants to have you worship Him
And spend some time with you.
So if you're sick or needing help
Please call me so we can pray;
If not, then I'll look forward to
Your presence next Lord's day!

With sympathy, there is nothing one can say or do
But just remember, God loves you,
And He'll keep you daily in His love
Till you meet with Him above!

Love of Celebration

Poems of Christmas and Easter

Christmas at Our House

Lou S. Davidson ©1970

Christmastime at our house
    Is lots and lots of fun
We gaily trim a Christmas tree
    And give gifts to everyone.

We send presents to the children
    Of our missionaries too
And with baking cakes and cookies
    There are lots of things to do!

We love to sing the carols
    That tell us Jesus came
To die and save each one by faith
    Believing in His name.

Then we have a birthday cake
    With a candle for each one
Who has Jesus in his heart
    Then we blow them out! What fun!

We sing "Happy Birthday, Jesus"
    And He is glad, I'm sure
We give Him back the life He saved,
    And vow to love *Him* more.

Christmas Celebration

Lou S. Davidson   © 2002

It's Jesus's Birthday—
                                 Look at the date!
Bring out the candles
                Let's CELEBRATE!
We can't surprise Him
                He knows our every deed
Or give Him presents
                There's nothing He would need.
But we can sing His praises
                And remember why He came,
We can meet the needs of others
                And do it in His name.

"Inasmuch as ye have done it unto one of
                the least of these, My brethren,
Ye have done it unto *Me*!" (Matt 25:40)

                Love and prayers to all.

Christmas Peace to You

Lou S. Davidson   ©1949

*The glory of the Lord shone round about
The angels sang praises to God,
And the star gave light in the darkened night
On the path the shepherds trod.*

*May the light from heaven guide your way,
May you know that "peace on earth,"
And your heart be filled with the Savior's love
As we celebrate His birth!*

Many years ago, I asked a group of young children, "Who's birthday is Christmas?" Several called out "Jesus's." Then I heard "Santa's!" I couldn't believe it.

About that time, a lady in Miami, where we lived at that time, tried to get people to have a birthday cake for Jesus. My first thought was "*Why not?*" That was about 1960.

Ever since then, we have had a birthday cake for Jesus, lit candles—one for each person present. Daddy said a prayer giving thanks to God for our Savior and all of our blessings, then we all sang "Happy Birthday" to Jesus. What a blessing!

Now, Daddy's with Jesus, and I have passed the torch to the children. What a blessing it was last week to have my daughter light the candles and my son-in-law say the prayer and lead the singing.

I'm sharing this, praying that others might adopt the practice for the future and be as blessed as we were.

Jesus's Birthday

Lou S. Davidson (c) 2001

They said it was my birthday and
The whole family came
They ate and opened gifts galore
But no one spoke my name

I thought I had the wrong address
So I went on my way
But to other homes I entered
It was just another day!

Then others said, "Come celebrate,
It's the day that Christ was born."
They drank and laughed and swore
I just sat there quite forlorn.

Then I heard the sound of carols
And was welcomed with such love!
Then they read the Christmas story
And prayed to God above.

They lit candles on my birthday cake
And as they always do,
Sang "Happy birthday, Jesus,
Happy birthday to *you*."

Merry Christmas Not Merry Xmas!

Lou S. Davidson   © 1965

Please don't cross *Christ* out of *Christmas*
    For *Christ* is the theme of the day:
In perfect love came from above
    To a manger bed of hay.

    Please don't cross *Christ* out of *Christmas*
        He came to die for you and me,
That all who believe, and *him* receive
        Might live eternally.

If we cross *Christ* out of *Christmas*
        We are forever lost in our sin;
No man could be sinless as *He*
        Or ever could cleanse us within.

    So don't cross *Christ* out of *Christmas*
        But bid *him* to enter your heart;
Take time to pray, ask *him* today
        And He will never depart.

    How we *love* the *Christ* of *Christmas*
        and pray that you do too.

    —Kenny, Lou, Joy, Donadeane, and Jeanette
      (who had a part in creating the rhyme.)

Our Christmas card for 1965

When I first saw *Christmas* written with an *X* instead of *Christ*, I said, "Why, they have crossed out the main part of the holiday!" I thought that Christians would rebut this, but instead I found what seemed like *everybody's doin' it!*

I decided to do something about it if only getting it out of my system by writing a poem about that for our usual Christmas greetings. Store-bought cards were "very 'spensive" so we usually made our own. The above was our Christmas card for 1965.

Our Christmas Message

Lou S. Davidson   © 1962

C	Christmas greetings, we send your way
H	have a joyful and happy day today
R	remembering the gift of God anew
I	in grateful hearts, redemption true.
S	sin can no longer now enslave us
T	'tis Christ alone—now come to save us!
I	in this past year, so blessed were we
S	since Christ has saved our children three.
B	both of us, our all have poured
O	on the altar of our Lord.
R	righteousness has conquered thus
N	now two of them have followed us!
T	to yield completely to His will
O	on His command, to go—be still.
D	delight and joy in every test,
A	as we rejoice, we now would pray
Y	your life might be as fully blessed!

—Kenny, Lou,
Joy, Donadeane, and Jeanette

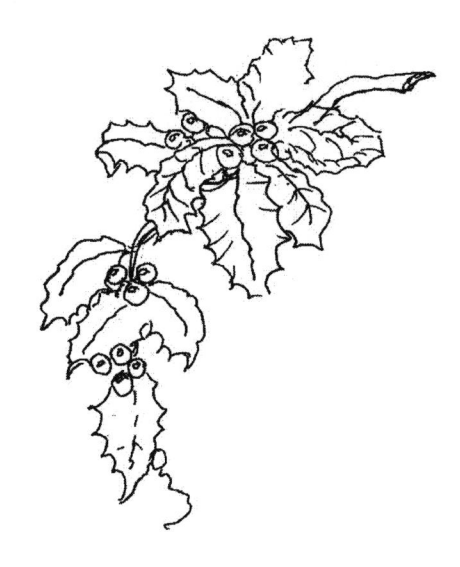

The First Christmas Gift

Lou S. Davidson   © 1992

The first Christmas gift
    Was for you and me
Found in a manger
    Not under a tree.

When God gave His Son
    For the souls of men
That through His death
    We are born again.

And our gift to Him
    On this Christmas day
Is to tell of His love
    To those on our way.

The Gift of Christmas

L. S. Davidson ©2005

As we gather to give gifts and joy
To others we hold dear;
Remembering the gift God gave
We celebrate each year!

He came in great humility
To give His life for me
That I may know His precious love
And from my sins be free.

So as we go from place to place
Our gifts and love to share
Let's not forsake God's wondrous gift
And show Him that we care.

The Good News

Lou S. Davidson   © 2001

Suppose they had not told them
Nor brought to them this joy—
Nor told them where they'd find Him
That holy baby boy!

With people all around us
We have the news to tell
He came to die for our sins;
To save us all from hell,

So thank the one who told you
Then go and tell another
Of Jesus Christ the Savior.
Because there is *no* other!

> 8: "And there were in the same country, shepherds abiding in the field keeping watch over their flock by night and the Angel of the Lord came upon them, and the glory of the Lord shone round about them, and they were sore afraid.
>
> 10: Behold, I bring you good tidings of great JOY which shall be to all people, for unto you is born this day—in the city of David, a Savior which is Christ, the Lord!
>
> And it came to pass, as the angels were gone away from them into heaven the shepherds said one to another, Let us now go even unto Bethlehem, and see this thing which is come to pass, which the Lord hath made known unto us!" (Luke 2:8-15)

Whenever I read this passage, I think, *Suppose they didn't want to leave their sheep and take that long trek? What about me?*

The Reason We Celebrate

Lou S. Davidson   ©2003

As we think of Christmas
    At the close of this year
We remember our friends
    And those we hold dear.

As we check off the cards
    And the gifts on our list
We make sure that not one
    Is omitted or missed!

Then when all is finished
    It's so often, I find
The One who made Christmas
    Has been left behind.

The real reason He came
    Was to die for our sin
When we opened our heart
    His Spirit came in.

So since it's His birthday
    With our love so sincere
Let's promise to serve Him
    Throughout the New Year.

The Story of Christmas

Lou S. Davidson © *1999*

He sat on high with the Father
Looking down on sinful man.
"Are You willing, my Son," the Father said,
"to carry out the plan?

"To go—be born as a baby,
Then to lead a sinless life,
To bear ridicule, hatred, rejection,
To suffer heartache and strife?"

"Are You willing to be tortured,
To die on a cross in pain?
Then spend three days in the heart of the earth
Ere You're raised to life again?"

"That all who ever hear of Thee
And in gratitude and love,
Request Your Spirit to dwell in their heart
May be welcomed here above?"

He was willing!

What Christmas Means to Me

Lou S. Davidson   © 1963

Not the red of a Santa Claus suit,
Nor the white of the driven snow;
But the blood that flowed from Calvary's cross
Where Jesus suffered so.

Not the gold of a synthetic tree,
But the crown that He left above
When He came to die for sinful man
In God's great plan of love.

Not the silver of tinkling bells
But the cross and the open grave!
For He came and died and rose again
Our sinful souls to save.

Not a season of frolic and sin
But a time of worship sincere,
With children and loved ones giving thanks
And singing songs of cheer.

Not the thought of an expensive gift,
But a prayer that each of you
Might receive the Christ of Christmas
To be your Savior too.

After He Rose

Luke 24: 36
Lou S. Davidson   © 1964

To prove Himself alive to them,
"Behold my hands," He said,
"Handle Me and see 'tis I
Now risen from the dead.

"Have ye here any meat to eat?"
While they not yet believed
He ate the fish and honeycomb
Their troubled hearts relieved.

Their understanding opened
He the scriptures quoth to them
That they must witness to the world
Beginning at Jerusalem.

Let's Celebrate!

Lou S. Davidson ©2000

He came to die for our sins
The price He fully paid
The stripes they laid upon His back
Should have on us been laid.

The tomb that could not hold Him
Was to show to us who care
And accept Him as our Savior
We'll meet Him in the air!

Unless He calls us sooner
Then He'll call us one by one
To meet Him up in heaven
And praise God for His Son!

"Believe on the Lord Jesus Christ,
and thou shalt be saved, and thy house" (Acts 16:31).

The Easter Story

Lou S. Davidson   © 1995

> I'm so glad He didn't come down
>   And save Himself as they cried . . .
>
> I'm so glad He didn't descend
>   But just suffered there and died!
>
> I'm so glad He didn't save himself
>   But died to set us free;
>
> I'm so glad that He arose again
>   That He might live in me!

As I read from Mark 15:29-30, I thought of the horrors of the cross and my Savior's crucifixion. As He was taunted by those around Him to do what *they* thought He couldn't do, surely this was the *true* last temptation of Christ. How glad I was that He did not *yield* to that temptation. For if He had, we would be without hope and without salvation, having to die and suffer for our own sins, which would not gain us the glorious eternity in heaven that He obtained for us there on the cross.

Even though it seemed hard to think, "I'm so *glad*," I must admit that *I am so glad* He died for my sins, that He arose again, and that *someone* prayed with me to receive what He did for me—for forgiveness of my sins, for the joy of my salvation, for the promise of eternal life in heaven. Now, I believe the greatest thing we can do to let Him know of our appreciation is to help others to pray this prayer and become believers and receivers too.

> Lord Jesus, I believe that You suffered and died for *my* sins, and I ask Thee to come into my heart and make me a *new creation*, a child of God, that I might know the joy of sins forgiven, and a new life.
>
> In the name of Christ, my Savior, *amen.*